PowerPoint 2019 Beginner

POWERPOINT ESSENTIALS 2019 BOOK 1

M.L. HUMPHREY

Copyright © 2021 M.L. Humphrey

All Rights Reserved.

ISBN: 978-1-63744-035-3

SELECT TITLES BY M.L. HUMPHREY

POWERPOINT ESSENTIALS 2019

PowerPoint 2019 Beginner

PowerPoint 2019 Intermediate

EXCEL ESSENTIALS 2019

Excel 2019 Beginner

Excel 2019 Intermediate

Excel 2019 Formulas & Functions

WORD ESSENTIALS 2019

Word 2019 Beginner

Word 2019 Intermediate

ACCESS ESSENTIALS 2019

Access 2019 Beginner

Access 2019 Intermediate

CONTENTS

Introduction	1
Basic Terminology	3
Absolute Basics	13
Your Workspace	21
Edit Presentation Slides	25
Presentation Themes	29
Slide Layouts	35
Add and Format Text	45
Format Paragraphs	61
Add Other Items To a Presentation Slide	73
Tables	75
Pictures	81
Animations	89
Design Principles	95
Other Tips and Tricks	99

CONTENTS (CONT.)

PRESENT YOUR SLIDES	105
PRINT YOUR PRESENTATION	109
WHERE TO LOOK FOR OTHER ANSWERS	117
CONCLUSION	119

Introduction

This guide focuses specifically on how to use Microsoft PowerPoint 2019. If you have an older version of PowerPoint, *PowerPoint for Beginners*, the predecessor to this book, is likely a better choice because it was written to be more generic and accessible to users of any version of PowerPoint from 2007 onward.

This guide, *PowerPoint 2019 Beginner*, just focuses on how to use Microsoft PowerPoint 2019. What that means, practically speaking, is that all screenshots in this book will be from PowerPoint 2019 and all instructions in this book will be written for users of PowerPoint 2019.

At the beginner level there really isn't a significant difference between the two books and you will likely be able to use either one to learn PowerPoint. You definitely do not need both of them.

Alright, then. Now that we have that out of the way.

The purpose of this guide is to introduce you to the basics of using Microsoft PowerPoint 2019, which is one of the go-to software programs for creating presentation slides. I've used it throughout my professional career and I know of a number of students who have also needed to use it for class presentations.

It is a fantastic tool, but if you've ever been on the receiving end of a consulting presentation, you likely also know how it can be misused by people who cram far too much information into a single slide for it to actually work as a presentation.

Same goes for if you've ever been subjected to someone who got a little too excited about the bells and whistles available through PowerPoint and created a presentation where every single page or bullet point whizzed and spun and danced onto the screen.

M.L. Humphrey

(As you can tell, I have opinions about proper presentations. To me a presentation should give enough information to prompt the speaker to remember what they need to say, but not be such a distraction that no one listens to the speaker. You want to write a report? Write a report. You want to have dancing, spinning, spiraling text? You better be in third grade.)

Anyway. PowerPoint is a useful and important program to learn. The goal for this book is to teach you enough of it that you can comfortably use one of the PowerPoint templates to create your own presentation which includes text, pictures, and/or tables of information.

You will also learn how to format any text you enter, how to add notes to your slides, how to animate your slides so that each bullet point appears separately, and how to launch your presentation as a slide show. We will also cover how to print a copy of your presentation as well as how to print handouts.

As you can see, I will also be sprinkling in my opinion throughout this guide so it isn't just going to be how to do things in PowerPoint but why you might want to do it in a certain way.

There are other aspects to PowerPoint that I'm not going to cover in this guide. For example, we're not going to discuss how to use SmartArt. Nor will we discuss how to insert charts or create a presentation from scratch. If you want to continue with your knowledge of PowerPoint, many of those topics are covered in *PowerPoint 2019 Intermediate*.

The goal of this guide is to give you enough information on how to create a basic presentation without overwhelming you with information you may not need. I will, however, end with a discussion of how to find help for any additional topics you need to learn. PowerPoint, just like Word and Excel, has a certain underlying logic to it and if you pay attention to that structure it's generally easy to find what you need when you need it.

There is definitely overlap between how things work in Word and Excel, so if you've already mastered one of those programs PowerPoint will be much easier for you to learn. But if you haven't, we'll cover what you need to know, don't worry.

Alright then. First things first, let's get started with some basic terminology.

Basic Terminology

Before we do anything else, I want to make sure that we're on the same page in terms of terminology. Some of this will be standard to anyone talking about these programs and some of it is my personal quirky way of saying things, so best to skim through if nothing else.

Tab

I refer to the menu choices at the top of the screen (File, Home, Insert, Design, Transitions, Animations, Slide Show, Review, View, etc.) as tabs. If you click on one you'll see that the way it's highlighted sort of looks like an old-time filing system.

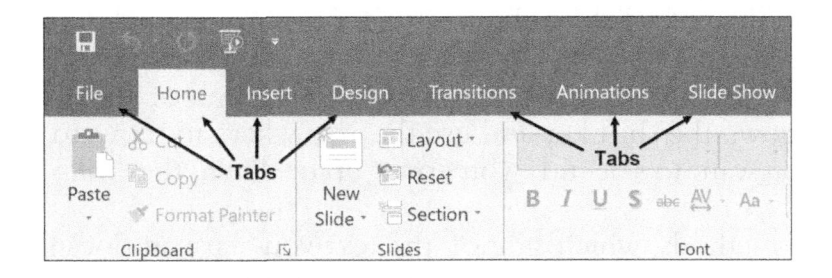

Each tab you select will show you different options. For example, in the image above, I have the Home tab selected and you can do various tasks such as cut/copy/paste, add new slides, change the slide layout, change fonts or font size or font color, change text formatting, add shapes, find/replace, etc. Other tabs will give other options.

3

Click

If I tell you to click on something, that means to use your mouse (or trackpad) to move the arrow on the screen over to a specific location and left-click or right-click on the option. (See the next definition for the difference between left-click and right-click).

If you left-click, this selects the item. If you right-click, this generally creates a dropdown list of options to choose from. If I don't tell you which to do, left- or right-click, then left-click.

Left-Click/Right-Click

If you look at your mouse or your trackpad, you generally have two flat buttons to press. One is on the left side, one is on the right. If I say left-click that means to press down on the button on the left. If I say right-click that means press down on the button on the right.

Now, as I sadly learned when I had to upgrade computers, not all trackpads have the left- and right-hand buttons. In that case, you'll basically want to press on either the bottom left-hand side of the trackpad or the bottom right-hand side of the trackpad. Since you're working blind it may take a little trial and error to get the option you want working. (Or is that just me?)

Select or Highlight

If I tell you to select text, that means to left-click at the end of the text you want to select, hold that left-click, and move your cursor to the other end of the text you want to select.

Another option is to use the Shift key. Go to one end of the text you want to select. Hold down the shift key and use the arrow keys to move to the other end of the text you want to select. If you arrow up or down, that will select an entire row at a time.

With both methods, which side of the text you start on doesn't matter. You can start at the end and go to the beginning or start at the beginning and go to the end. Just start at one end or the other of the text you want to select.

The text you've selected will then be highlighted in gray.

If you need to select text that isn't touching you can do this by selecting your first section of text and then holding down the Ctrl key and selecting your second section of text using your mouse.

Basic Terminology

(You can't arrow to the second section of text or you'll lose your already selected text.)

To select an object, you can generally just left-click on it. To select multiple objects, hold down the Ctrl key as you click on each object.

To select everything in your workspace, you can use Ctrl + A. (This is a control shortcut, which we'll define in a moment.)

Dropdown Menu

If you right-click on a PowerPoint slide, you will see what I'm going to refer to as a dropdown menu. (Sometimes it will actually drop upward if you're towards the bottom of the document.)

A dropdown menu provides you a list of choices to select from like this one that appears when I right-click on a presentation slide:

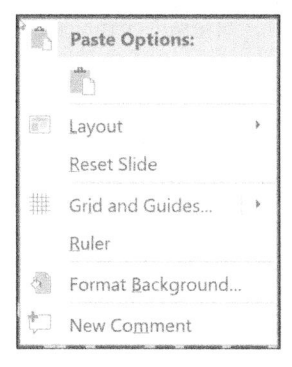

```
Paste Options:
Layout          ▶
Reset Slide
Grid and Guides... ▶
Ruler
Format Background...
New Comment
```

There are also dropdown menus available for some of the options listed under the tabs at the top of the screen. For example, if you go to the Home tab, you'll see small arrows below or next to some of the options, like the Layout option and the Section option in the Slides section. Clicking on those little arrows will give you a dropdown menu with a list of choices to choose from like this one for Section:

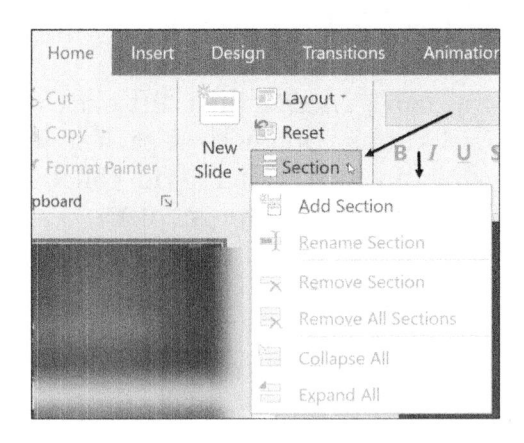

Expansion Arrows

I don't know the official word for these, but you'll also notice at the bottom right corner of most of the sections in each tab that there are little arrows pointing down and to the right.

If you click on one of those arrows PowerPoint will bring up a more detailed set of options, usually through a dialogue box (which we'll discuss next) or a task pane (which we'll discuss after that).

In the Home tab, for example, there are expansion arrows for Clipboard, Font, Paragraph, and Drawing. Holding your mouse over the arrow will give a brief description of what clicking on the expansion arrow will do like here for the Clipboard section on the Home tab where it tells you that clicking on the expansion arrow will allow you to see all items that have been copied to the clipboard.

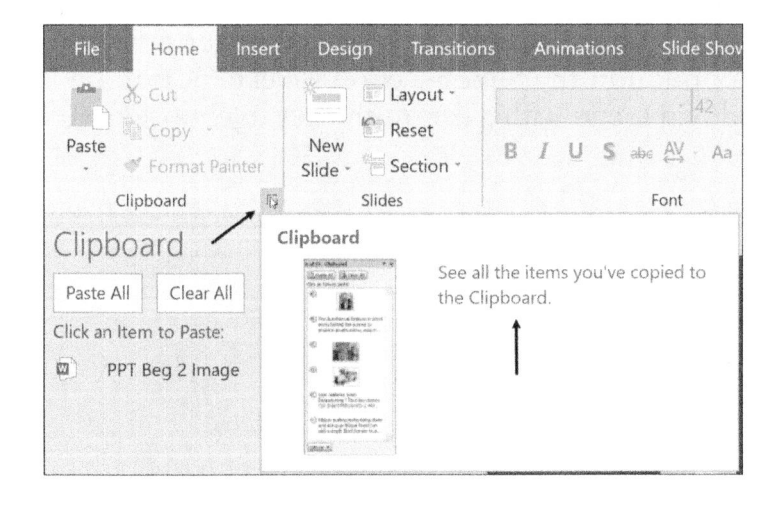

Basic Terminology

In this instance, clicking on the expansion arrow opens a task pane on the left-hand side of the screen, which is visible in the background of the image above.

Dialogue Box

Dialogue boxes are pop-up boxes that cover specialized settings. As just mentioned, if you click on an expansion arrow, it will often open a dialogue box that contains more choices than are visible in that section.

Also, if you right-click on the text in a PowerPoint content slide and choose Font, Paragraph, or Hyperlink from the dropdown menu that will open a dialogue box.

Dialogue boxes often allow the most granular level of control over an option. For example, this is the Font dialogue box which you can see has more options available than in the Font section of the Home tab.

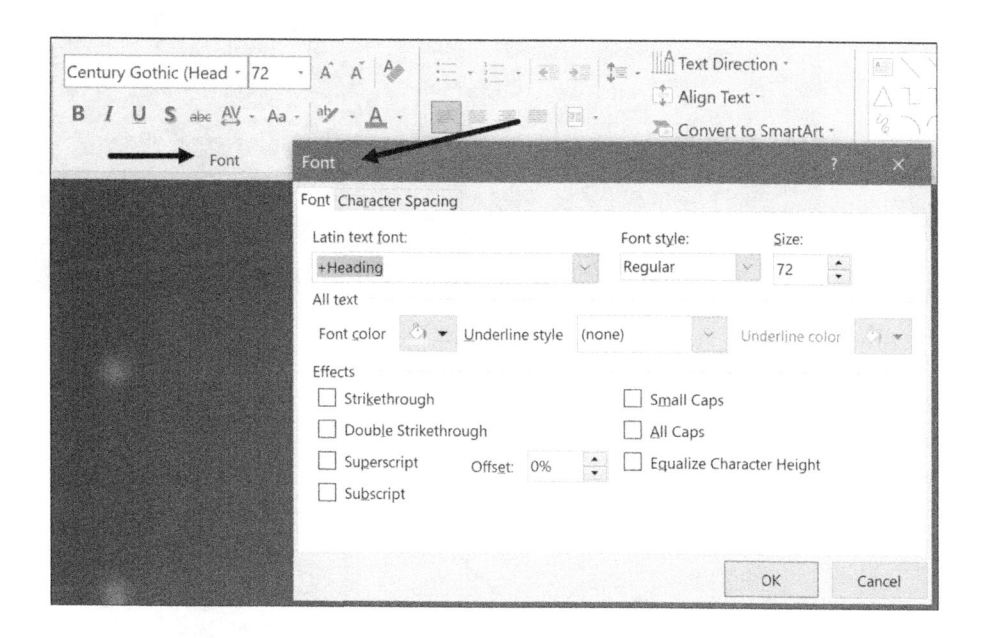

Task Pane

What I refer to as task panes are separate work spaces that are visible to the left- and right-hand sides of your main workspace. They may also occasionally appear below your main workspace.

7

M.L. Humphrey

For example, When you first open PowerPoint, there will generally be a task pane on the left-hand side that shows thumbnail images of the slides in your presentation. This is an area you can navigate in separate from your main workspace.

Here is an example of a business presentation template I opened with the slides in a task pane to the left and the title slide in the main workspace:

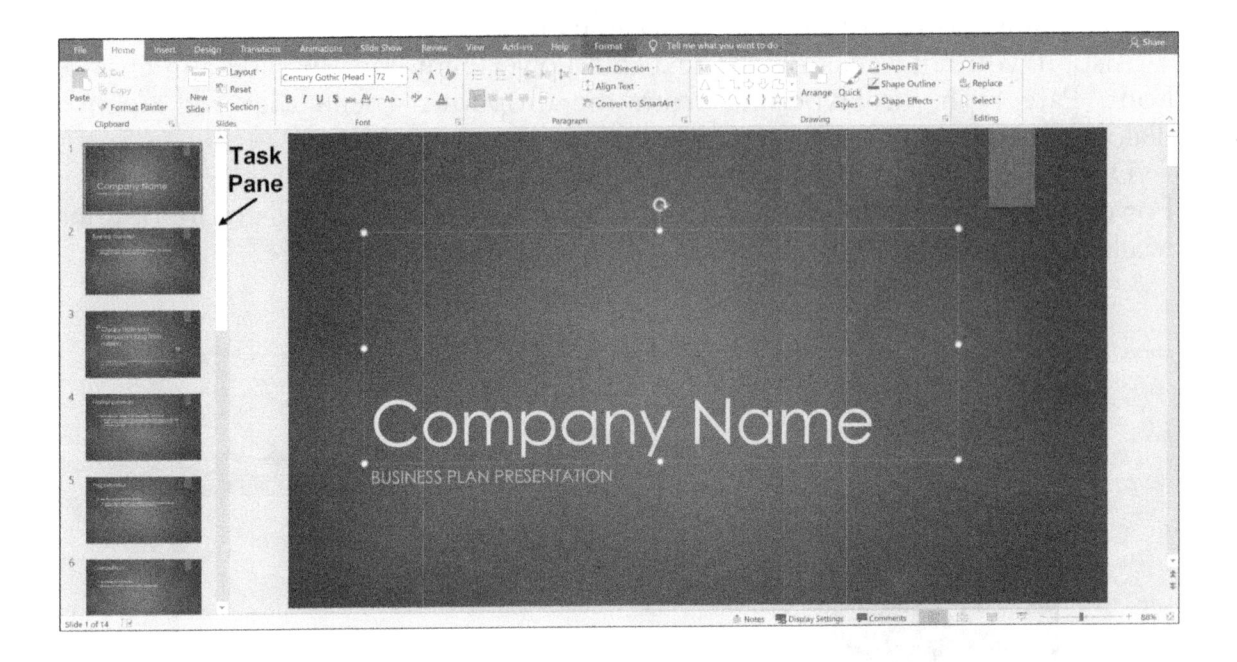

You can have multiple task panes open at once. To close a task pane that is not permanently visible, such as the Clipboard task pane, click on the X in the top right corner.

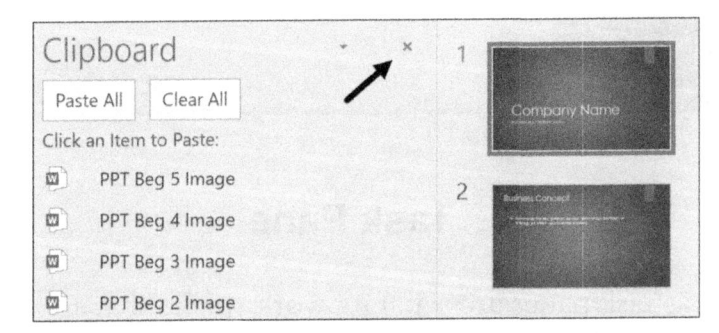

You can also click on the arrow next to the X and choose Close.

8

Basic Terminology

You can sometimes also move a task pane. To do so, click on the arrow in the top right corner and choose Move from the dropdown menu. That will detach the task pane from its current position. You can then left-click and drag the task pane to where you'd like.

To attach a task pane to the left-hand or right-hand side of the workspace, drag it off of the edge of the screen until it "docks" into place.

If you do move a task pane and then close it, when you reopen the task pane it will appear in the location you moved it to.

Scroll Bar

Scroll bars allow you to see content that isn't currently visible on the screen. PowerPoint usually has multiple scroll bars visible.

One scroll bar will appear on the right-hand side of the task pane that contains thumbnails of your presentation slides. This scroll bar lets you see the thumbnails of all available slides in the presentation by scrolling up and down.

Here is the top portion of that scroll bar:

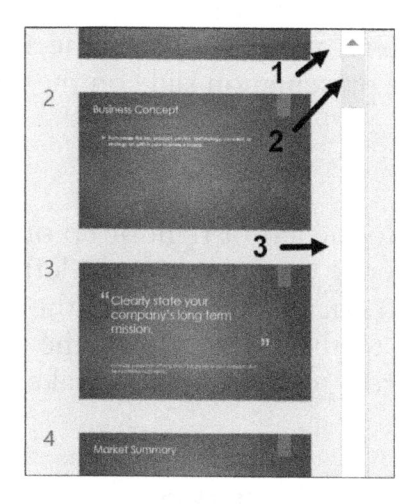

You can click on the up arrow (labeled 1) at the top or the down arrow (not visible here) at the bottom to move a small amount up or down.

If you click on the gray space above or below the scroll bar (labeled 2) that will move you one whole screen at a time. So if Slides 1 through 6 are currently visible, clicking below the scroll bar will make Slides 7 through 12 visible.

Or you can left-click on the scroll bar itself (labeled 3) and drag up or down to move through the available space at your own speed.

I personally tend to left-click and drag the scroll bar because that gives me the most control while still moving through my available slides at a relatively fast pace.

Another scroll bar will generally appear on the right-hand side of the main workspace. This scrollbar will by default let you navigate through each of the slides in your presentation one-by-one.

In the main workspace, there are a few more options. At the bottom of the scroll bar, you have a double up arrow and a double down arrow which can be clicked on to move to the previous slide or the next slide.

When you're at a normal zoom level, you will get that same result by clicking on the gray space above or below the scroll bar or on the arrows at the top or bottom of the scroll bar.

(If you increase the zoom level on your main workspace the scroll bar will instead move through portions of your slides.)

Generally, I don't use the scroll bar for the main workspace because I click onto the thumbnails in the left-hand task pane to move to the slide I want. Or to see an entire presentation one slide at a time I go into Slide Show mode, which we'll discuss later.

You won't normally see a scroll bar at the bottom of the screen, but it is possible. This would happen if you ever change the zoom level to the point that you're not seeing the entire presentation slide on the screen.

Arrow

If I ever tell you to arrow to the left or right or up or down, that just means use your arrow keys. This will move your cursor to the left one space, to the right one space, up one line, or down one line. If you're at the end of a line and arrow to the right, it will take you to the beginning of the next line. If you're at the beginning of a line and arrow to the left, it will take you to the end of the last line.

Cursor

There are two possible meanings for cursor. One is the one I just used. When you're clicked into a PowerPoint slide, you will see that there is a blinking line. This indicates where you are in the document. If you type text, each letter will appear where the cursor was at the time you typed it. The cursor will move (at least in the U.S. and I'd assume most European versions) to the right as you type. This version of the cursor should be visible at all times when you're clicked onto text.

Basic Terminology

The other type of cursor is the one that's tied to the movement of your mouse or trackpad. If you've clicked onto your text, the cursor will look somewhat like a tall skinny capital I when positioned over text. Move it up to the menu options or off to the sides, and it will generally become a white arrow or four-sided black arrow.

Usually I won't refer to your cursor, I'll just say, "click" or "select" or whatever action you need to take with it, and moving the cursor to that location will be implied.

Quick Access Toolbar

In the very top left corner of your screen above the Home tab, you should see a series of symbols. These are part of the Quick Access Toolbar. By default it appears to have options for Save, Undo, Redo, and Start from Beginning.

To see what each symbol stands for, hold your mouse over it and help text will appear.

You can customize what options appear there by clicking on the downward pointing arrow with a line above it located at the end of the line of symbols.

Click on any command you want that isn't currently visible to select it or click on one you no longer want to unselect it. The checkmarks next to each item indicate which are visible. For example, here the Save command is checked but none of the others are.

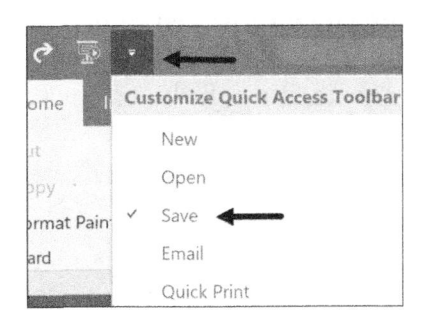

The Quick Access Toolbar can be useful if there's something you're doing repeatedly that's located on a different tab than something else you're doing repeatedly.

Control Shortcut

Throughout this document, I'm going to mention various control shortcuts that you can use to perform tasks like save, copy, cut, and paste like I did above with Select All, Ctrl +A.

Each of these will be written as Ctrl + a capital letter.

When you use the shortcut you do not need to use the capitalized version of the letter. For example, holding down the Ctrl key and the s key at the same time will save your document. I'll write this as Ctrl + S, but that just means hold down the key that says ctrl and the s key at the same time.

Undo

One of the most powerful control shortcuts in PowerPoint is the Undo option. If you do something you didn't mean or that you want to take back, use Ctrl + Z. This will reverse whatever you just did.

If you need to reverse more than one item, you can keep using Ctrl + Z until you've undone everything you wanted to undo, or you can use the Undo option in the Quick Access Toolbar.

If you use the Quick Access Toolbar there is a dropdown menu option that lets you choose to undo multiple steps at once.

Either way, though, you have to undo things in order. So if I bold, underline, and italicize text and want to undo the bolding on the text, I would also have to undo the italics and underline since those happened after I bolded the text. I can't choose to just undo the bolding. Undo walks you backwards one thing at a time.

(Which is why in that example, it might be easier to just unbold the text rather than try to use undo.)

Absolute Basics

Now let's discuss some absolute basics, like opening, closing, saving, and deleting presentations.

Start a New PowerPoint Presentation

To start a brand new PowerPoint presentation, I choose PowerPoint from my applications menu or click on the shortcut I have on my computer's taskbar. If you're already in PowerPoint and want to start a new PowerPoint presentation you can go to the File tab and choose New from the left-hand menu.

You can also use Ctrl + N to start a new presentation. That will bring up a Title Slide that has no theme and is just plain white.

Using the File→New option will give you a choice of a number of different presentations that are pre-formatted. The blank presentation option is also available, but I recommend using one of the pre-formatted options when you can since they've already thought through complementary colors and imagery and font choices.

Clicking on any of the themes will bring up a secondary display. You can actually use the arrows on the left- and right-hand sides of that display to navigate through the template choices and see a little description related to each template.

For some of the templates there will be variant versions shown. For example, for me if I click on the Circuit presentation template it shows that there are four color palettes available. I can click on any of the four variants to use that color palette. Here I've clicked on the gray option instead of the blue:

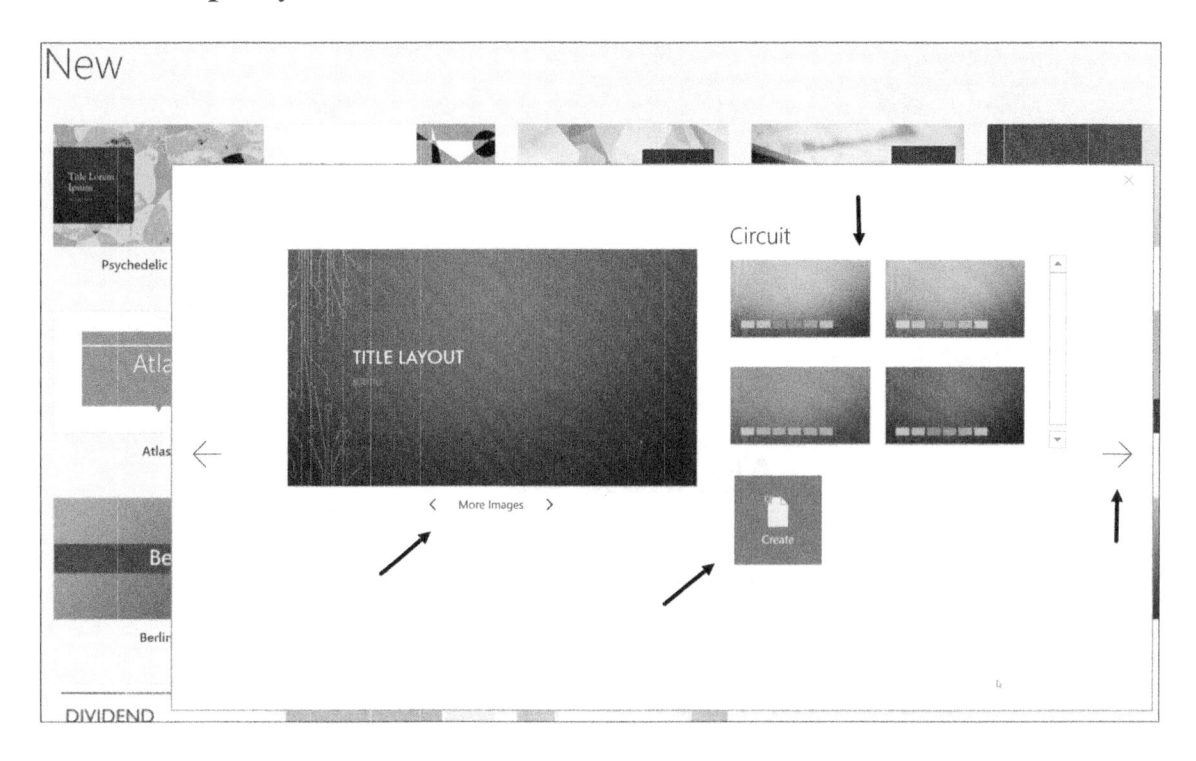

Also, some of the templates may have a More Images option underneath the title slide image. You can click on the arrows there to see what the interior slide layouts for that template will look like.

This can be important because, for example, if you're going to print a presentation chances are you don't want the main presentation slides to use a colored background. You'll want to instead use a template like Ion Boardroom that has a white background on the main presentation slides.

And don't worry if you choose a "bad" template initially. You can change the template and the variant on that template later if you realize the template you chose isn't going to work for you.

Okay, then.

Once you've found a template you like, click on it and then on Create to have PowerPoint start a draft presentation for you to work from.

The presentation should appear with a Title page that has draft text showing on it, usually "Click to Add Title" and often "Click to Add Subtitle."

As I mentioned above, you can always choose a template after you've started working on your presentation using the Design tab which we'll cover later. But if you chose a blank presentation using Ctrl + N you will also have a Design Ideas task pane appear.

Absolute Basics

    I wouldn't recommend using one of the options from the Design Ideas task pane, though, because as far as I can tell it only provides you with a style for the title slide and not the rest of the presentation.

    I don't see a way to then have the rest of the slides in your presentation match that title slide style. So the rest of your presentation would still be plain white with black text if you chose one of those options, which isn't very helpful.

    Okay, then. That's how to start a brand new presentation. If you have a corporate template you're working from, chances are you'll need to use that instead, so let's talk about how to open an existing presentation next.

Open an Existing PowerPoint File

To open an existing PowerPoint file you can go to the folder where the file is saved and double-click on the file name. Or you can open PowerPoint without selecting a file and it will provide a list of recent documents to choose from under the Recent heading in the middle of the screen.

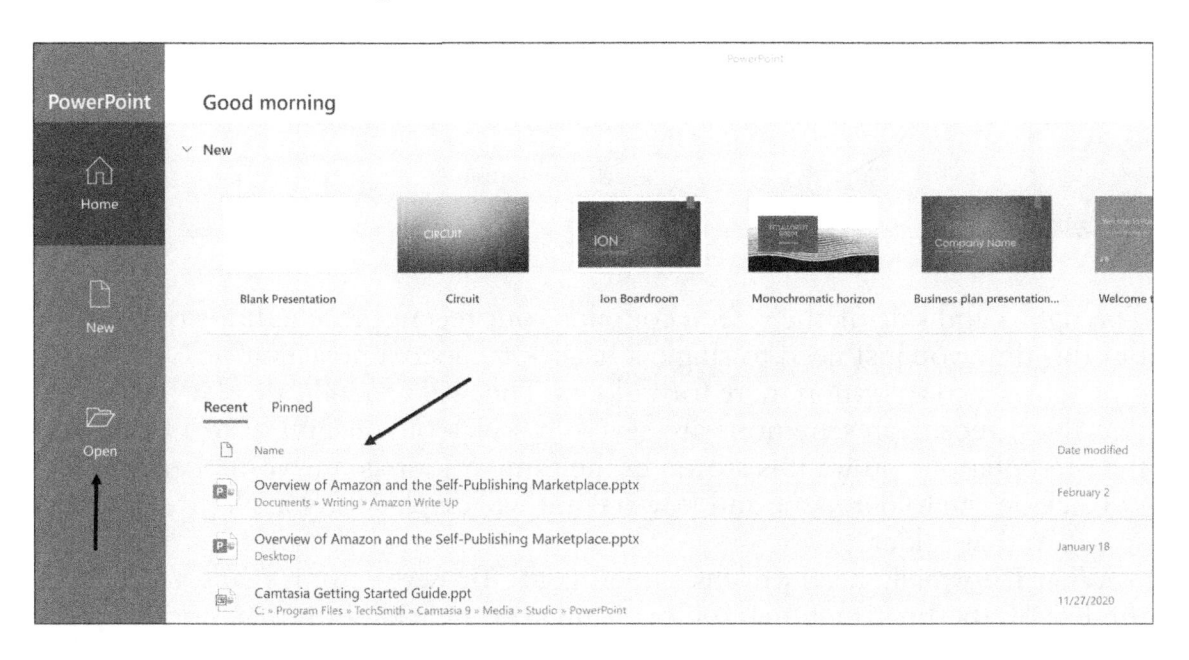

Double-click on one of those file names and the presentation will open.

    Next to the Recent heading is a Pinned heading. If you have any presentations that you always want to be able to access easily you can pin them and no matter how long it's been since you opened that presentation last you'll be able to find it under the Pinned heading.

15

To pin a file, single-click on its name under Recent and look to the right-hand side of the listing. There should be a small thumbtack image. Click on that and the file will be added to the Pinned section.

To unpin a file, just click on the thumbtack again.

If you're in PowerPoint and don't see the file you want under either Recent or Pinned, you can either click on More Presentations at the bottom of the recent files listing or click on the Open option on the left-hand sidebar. Both will bring you to the Open screen.

You can also reach the screen by using Ctrl + O.

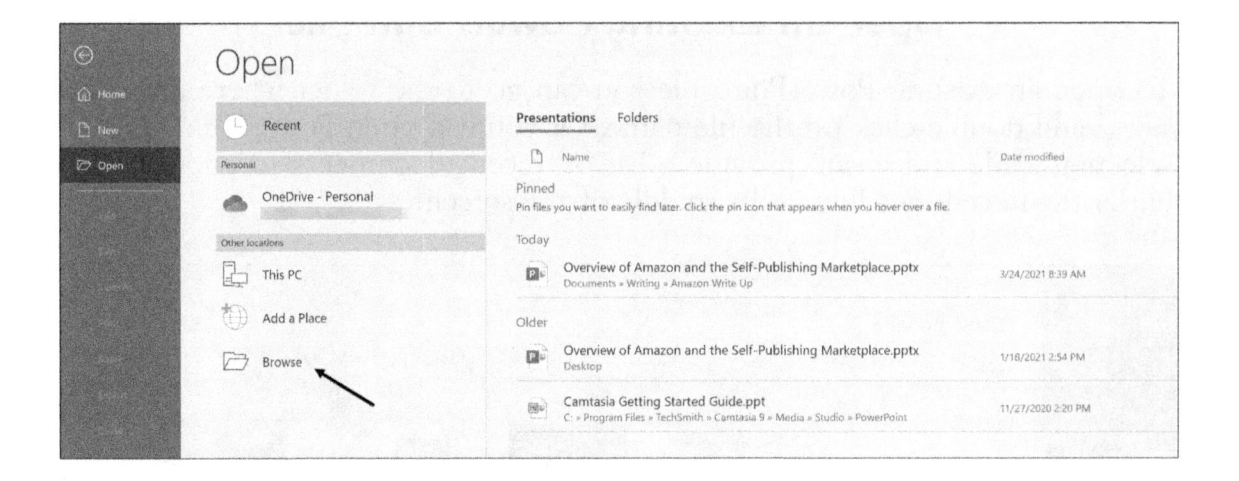

The right-hand side of the screen contains your recent presentations once more, but this time you just need to single left-click to open a presentation.

There is also an option there for Folders. This will generally display the folders that those recent presentations are saved in so it's only useful if you know that the presentation you want is stored in the same folder as one you recently used.

Click on the folder name and PowerPoint will display for you all presentations stored in that folder.

What I normally need on this screen is the Browse option that's available to the left of the presentations/folders listing. Left-clicking on that brings up the Open dialogue box which allows you to navigate to any location on your computer. Mine by default opens to the Documents folder.

Once you find the file you want, either click on it and then choose Open, or double-click on it.

Absolute Basics

Save a PowerPoint File

To quickly save your presentation, you can use Ctrl + S or click on the small image of a floppy disk in the Quick Access Toolbar.

For a document you've already saved that will overwrite the prior version of the document with the current version and will keep the file name, file type, and file location the same.

If you need to change the file name, type, or location you'll need to use the Save As option instead. This can be accessed via the File tab.

(With respect to file type, I sometimes need to, for example, save a presentation as a .pdf or a .jpg file instead.)

When you use Save As you wil need to navigate to where you want to save your file by either clicking on one of the listed file names or by clicking on one of the locations on the left-hand side.

Here I've clicked on Browse which opens a Save As dialogue box that shows the default name PowerPoint assigned, the default file type, and which shows my Documents folder so that I can navigate to where I want to save the file.

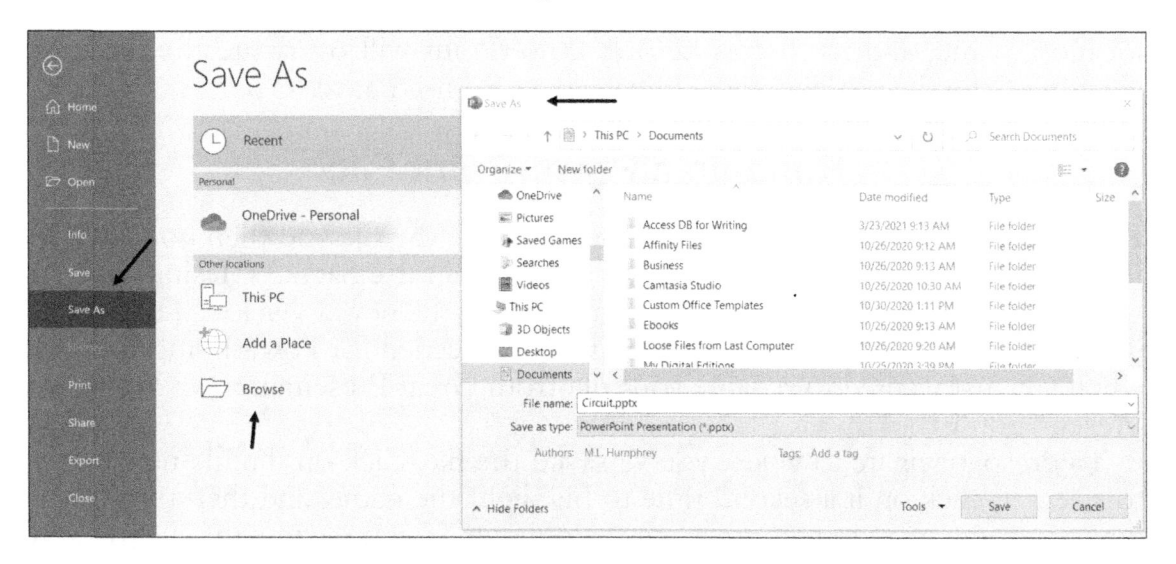

There are still defaults for name and format, but you'll want to change the name of the document to something better than the template name.

If you try to save a file that has never been saved before, it will automatically default to the Save As option and open a dialogue box which requires that you specify where to save the file and what to name it.

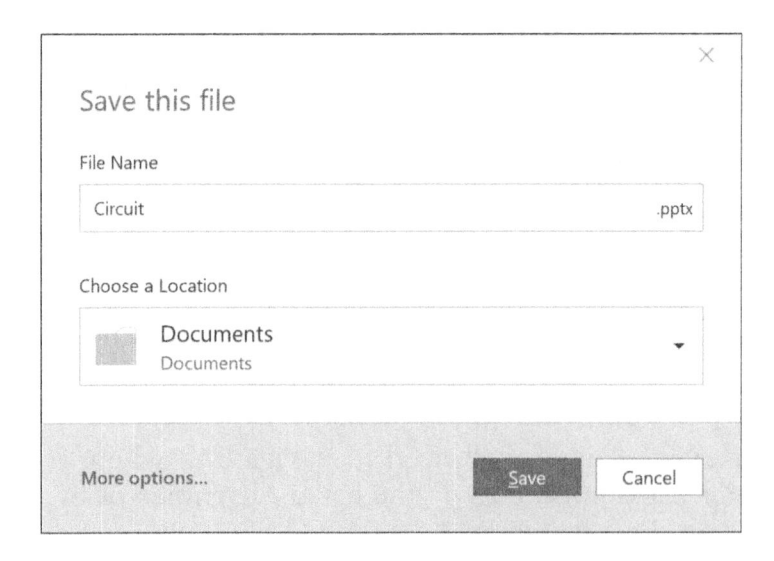

Clicking on More Options will let you also change the file type before you save. It does so by taking you to the Save As screen.

If you had already saved the file and you choose to Save As but keep the same location, name, and format as before, PowerPoint will overwrite the previous version of the file just like it would have if you'd used Save.

Rename a PowerPoint File

If you just want to rename a file, it's best to close the file and then go to where the file is saved and rename it that way rather than use Save As. Using Save As will keep the original of the file as well as creating the newer version. That's great when you want version control (which is rarely needed for PowerPoint), but not when you just wanted to rename your file from Great Presentation v22 to Great Presentation FINAL.

To do so, navigate to where you've saved the file, click on the file name once to select it, click on it a second time to highlight the name, and then type in the new name you want to use, replacing the old one. If you rename the file this way outside of PowerPoint, there will only be one version of the file left, the one with the new name you wanted.

Just be aware that if you rename a file by navigating to where it's located and changing the name you won't be able to access the file from the Recent Presentations list under Open since that will still list the old name which no longer exists. The next time you want to open that file you'll need to navigate to where it's stored and open it that way.

Delete a PowerPoint File

You can't delete a PowerPoint file from within PowerPoint. You need to close the file you want to delete and then navigate to where the file is stored and delete the file from there without opening it.

To do so, locate the file and click on the file name. (Only enough to select it. Make sure you haven't double-clicked and highlighted the name which will delete the file name but not the file.) Next, choose Delete from the menu at the top of the screen, or right-click and choose Delete from the dropdown menu.

Close a PowerPoint File

To close a PowerPoint file click on the X in the top right corner or go to File and then choose Close. (You can also use Ctrl + W, but I never have.)

If no changes have been made to the document since you saved it last, it will just close.

If changes have been made, PowerPoint should ask you if you want to save those changes. You can either choose to save them, not save them, or cancel closing the document and leave it open. I almost always default to saving any changes. If I'm in doubt about whether I'd be overwriting something important, I cancel and choose to Save As and save the current file as a later version of the document just in case (e.g., Great Presentation v2).

If you had copied an image or a large block of text before trying to close your presentation, you may also have a dialogue box pop up asking if you want to keep that image or text available for use when you close the document. Usually the answer to this is no, but if you had planned on pasting that image or text somewhere else and hadn't yet done so, you can say to keep it on the clipboard.

**

Okay. Now let's talk about your workspace. We touched on it a bit when we defined task panes, but I want to go over it in more detail now.

Your Workspace

Whether you choose to start a brand new file or open an existing file, you'll end up in the main workspace for PowerPoint. It looks something like this:

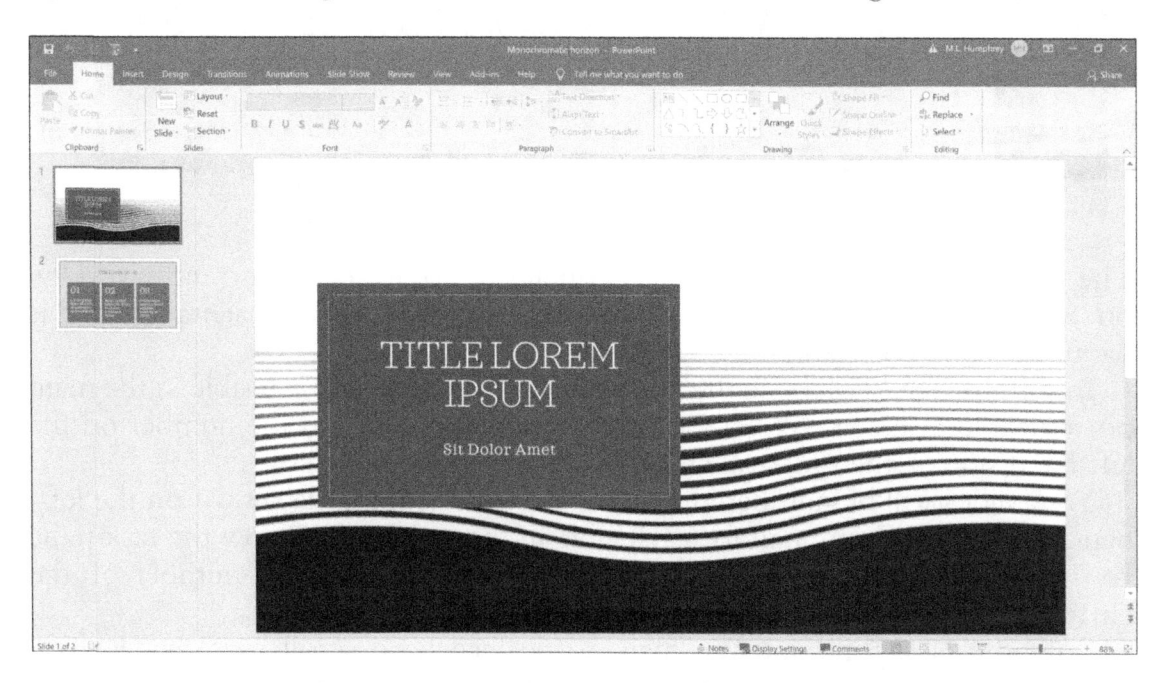

We'll walk through this in more detail in the Working with Your Presentation Slides section but I just wanted you to see right now that there's a left-hand task pane that shows all of the slides in the presentation and then a main section of the screen that shows the slide you're currently working on.

For a new presentation there's usually just the one title slide. This one happens to have two slides that it opens with.

The business presentation template opens with fourteen slides. Let's look through that one now:

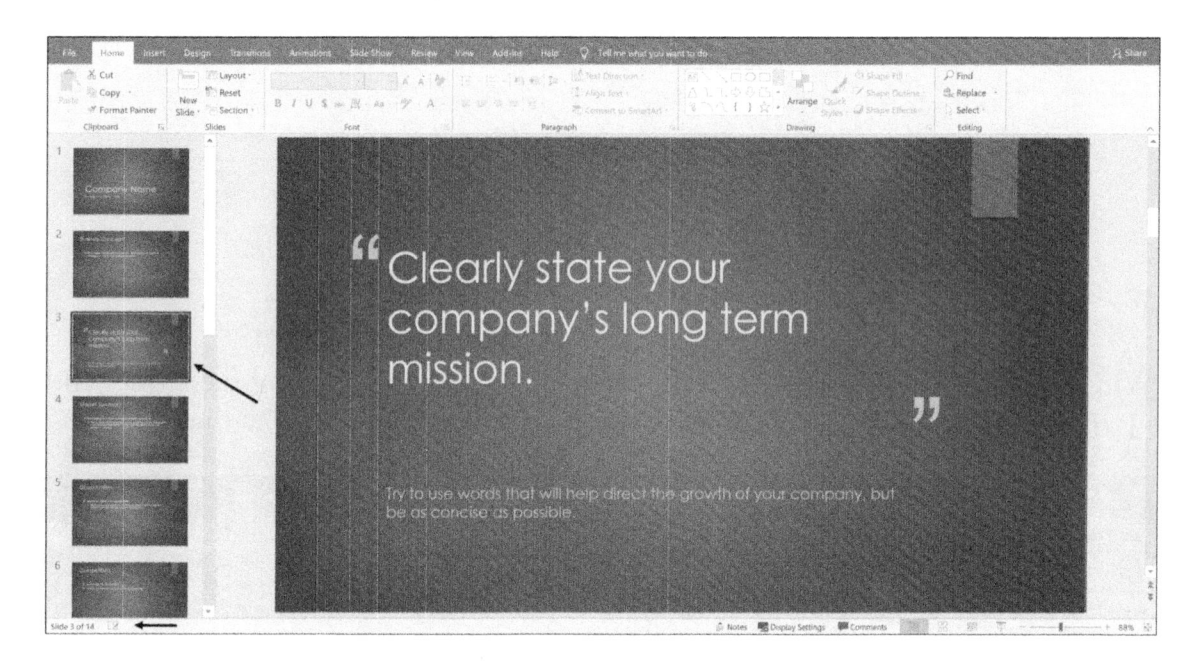

The main portion of the screen will contain the slide you're currently working on. So in this case I've selected a slide from farther into the presentation that is a Quote Name Card slide.

In the left-hand task pane the thumbnail of the slide that is visible in the main portion of the screen will have a dark border around it and the number on the left-hand side of the slide will also be colored a different color.

Your slides will be numbered starting at 1. The number is shown on the left-hand side of the thumbnail for each slide in the task pane. Below the task pane you can see how many slides are in the presentation and the number of the current slide. So here that says 3 of 14.

Both the task pane and the main workspace have scroll bars that let you navigate through the presentation. To move to a different slide you can also double-click on its thumbnail in the task pane and it will appear in the main workspace.

In the bottom right corner you can also change the zoom level for the main workspace. (I usually leave that alone, though.)

Your Workspace

Across the top of the workspace are your menu tabs which you may need to use when formatting the text or appearance of your presentation.

There are also dropdown menus available in both the task pane and the main workspace. In the task pane dropdown you have the options to cut, copy, paste, add a new slide, duplicate a slide, delete a slide, add a section (which is an intermediate-level topic), change the slide layout, and more. These relate to the slides themselves.

In the main workspace you also have a dropdown with cut, copy, and paste options, but these generally relate to the text on a slide. There are also options for font, paragraph, bullets, numbering, and more.

We'll revisit some of this later, but for now let's focus on that left-hand task pane and what you can do there with respect to your slides.

Edit Presentation Slides

Before we continue I want to edit your presentation slides, most of which is done by working in the left-hand slide task pane.

Add a Slide

If you right-click into the blank space below your slide(s) in the left-hand task pane, you'll see a dropdown menu that includes the New Slide option.

Click on that and PowerPoint will add a new slide to your presentation. The layout of the slide will either match the layout of the slide directly above it or will be a Title and Content slide if the slide directly above it was a Title slide.

You can also right-click on an existing slide and choose New Slide from that dropdown menu as well. If you do that, the slide that is added to your presentation will have the same layout as the one you right-clicked on.

Another option is to go to the Slides section of the Home tab and click on New Slide there. If you add a slide via the Home tab and click on the New Slide dropdown arrow you can choose the layout you want. (See the chapter on slide layouts for a discussion of the various layout options.)

Select a Slide or Slides

To select a single slide, you simply left-click on the slide where it's visible in the left-hand slide task pane. When a slide is selected it should have a darker border around it. In my version that border appears to be a dark red.

If you want to select more than one slide, left-click on the first slide and then hold down the Ctrl key as you left-click on the other slides you want.

Each selected slide will have that dark border around it.

Slides do not need to be next to one another for you to select them this way.

If you have a range of slides that you want to select, you can use the Shift key instead. Click on the slide at the top or the bottom of the range of slides you want, hold down the Shift key, and then click on the slide at the other end of the range of slides you want. All slides within that range, including both of the slides you clicked, will be selected.

(You can also combine methods of selecting slides to, for example, select a range of slides using Shift and then select an additional slide using the Ctrl key.)

No matter how many slides you select, the main workspace will only show one of them.

To remove your selection of multiple slides, click in the gray area around any of the slides or into your main workspace.

Move a Slide or Slides

The easiest way to move a slide or slides to a different position within your presentation is to select the slide(s) (as noted above) and then left-click and drag the slide(s) to the new location using the left-hand slide task pane.

As you move your chosen slide(s) you'll see the slides moving upward or downward to leave a space for your slide(s) to be inserted.

If you're moving more than one slide, you can left-click on any of the slides you've selected and drag.

All of the selected slides will move to the new location even if they weren't next to one another before.

As you move multiple slides at once you'll see a number in the top right corner telling you how many slides you're moving.

Cut a Slide or Slides

Cutting a slide removes it from its current location but lets you paste that slide elsewhere.

In the task pane, you can right-click on your chosen slide(s) and choose Cut from the dropdown menu. Or you can select your slide(s) and then use Ctrl + X. Or you can select your slide(s) and then go to the Clipboard section of the Home tab and choose Cut from there.

Any of these options will remove the slide(s) from their current position but let you paste them either into another location in that presentation or into another presentation altogether. (Usually within the same presentation I'd just

Edit Presentation Slides

move the slides, but if it was a very long presentation it might be easier to cut and paste instead.)

Copy a Slide or Slides

Copying a slide keeps that slide in its current position but takes a copy of the slide that you can then paste elsewhere.

In the left-hand task pane, you can right-click on your chosen slide(s) and choose Copy from the dropdown menu. Or you can select your slide(s) and then use Ctrl + C. Or you can select your slide(s) in the task pane and then go to the Clipboard section of the Home tab and choose Copy from there.

You also have a Duplicate option in PowerPoint which will take a copy of your selected slide(s) and immediately paste that copy below the selected slide(s). It's available if you right-click or if you click on the dropdown arrow next to Copy in the Clipboard section of the Home tab.

This means you only need to use Copy if you want to paste your copied slide(s) elsewhere in your document or into another presentation.

Paste a Slide or Slides

If you copy or cut a slide or slides and want to use them elsewhere, you need to paste them into that new location.

You can do a basic paste by clicking into the space where you want to put those slides (so between two existing slides or in the gray space at the end of the presentation, for example) and using Ctrl + V.

If you are clicked onto a slide when you use Ctrl + V, your copied or cut slides will be pasted in below that slide you were clicked onto.

You can also right-click where you want to paste a slide and choose from the paste options in the dropdown menu.

The first option, which has a small a in the bottom right corner, is Use Destination Theme. If you're cutting or copying and pasting within an existing presentation this won't mean much. I have used this one, however, when working with a corporate PowerPoint template where someone had drafted their presentation slides without using the template and I had to bring their content into the corporate template.

In a situation like that you can copy all of the slides from the initial version of the presentation and paste them into the corporate template using the destination theme option which will convert the slides from whatever theme was initially used to the corporate theme. You'll still have to walk through your document and make sure nothing was impacted by the change of theme, but at

27

least you won't have to change each slide's theme individually.

The second paste option you have, the one with the paintbrush in the bottom right corner, is Keep Source Formatting. This does exactly what it says, it keeps the formatting that the slide(s) already had.

Sometimes it's important to do this especially if you've done a lot of custom work on a slide and don't want your images, charts, etc. resized when you move them into a new presentation.

The third paste option, the one with a photo icon in the bottom right corner, is to paste a slide in as a Picture. That means the slide can no longer be edited. It's like someone took a snapshot of that slide and now you just have that snapshot. If you try to use this option with multiple slides only the first slide will paste in.

You can also paste slides by going to the Clipboard section of the Home tab and choosing Paste from there. The more advanced paste options are available by clicking on the arrow under Paste.

Delete a Slide

To delete a slide, you can click on that slide in the left-hand task pane and then hit the Delete or Backspace key. Either one will work. Or you can right-click on that slide and choose Delete Slide from the dropdown menu.

Reset a Slide

If you make changes to the layout of a slide, by for example changing the size of the text boxes or their location, and want to go back to the original layout for that slide type for that theme, you can right-click on the slide and choose Reset Slide from the dropdown menu. According to PowerPoint, this will "reset the position, size, and formatting of the slide placeholders to their default settings."

You can also do so by clicking on the slide you want to reset and clicking on the Reset option in the Slides section of the Home tab.

Presentation Themes

As a beginner, I highly recommend that you work with the presentation themes that PowerPoint provides you rather than trying to create a presentation from scratch. Presentation themes are pre-built to use colors, fonts, and imagery that all work together to provide a polished appearance.

As a matter of fact, the rest of this guide will assume that that's what you're doing. I do not cover here how to create a presentation from scratch.

We already covered above under how to create a new presentation how to start your presentation using one of the PowerPoint themes or a variation on that theme. This chapter will cover how to change your presentation theme once you've started to create your presentation.

There are a number of reasons why you might want to do so. For example, the audiences I've presented to in the past expect the title field on each slide to appear at the top of the slide. There are a handful of PowerPoint themes that place the title portion of the slide elsewhere. So if I were to inadvertently select one of those as I started to prepare, I'd need to change it once I realized that.

Also, some of the themes include a wider variety of slide layouts than others. If I knew I'd be using a certain slide layout that wasn't available in my chosen theme it might be easier to switch to a theme that did have that slide layout rather than try to create it myself.

So. How do you do this? How do you change your theme once you've started working on a presentation?

First, go to the Design tab.

You should see that the Themes section takes up most of the tab starting on the left-hand side of the screen. The first thumbnail in that section is your current theme followed by your other choices.

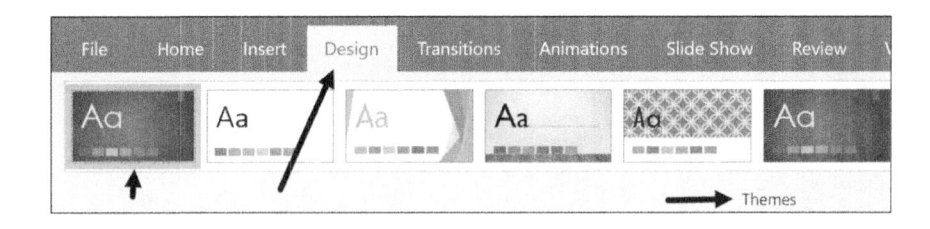

To see how each theme will look, you can hold your mouse over the thumbnail for that theme and PowerPoint will temporarily apply it to the slide in your main workspace.

To see more themes, click on the down arrow at the end. To see all themes at once, click on the down arrow with a line above it. That will give you something that looks like this:

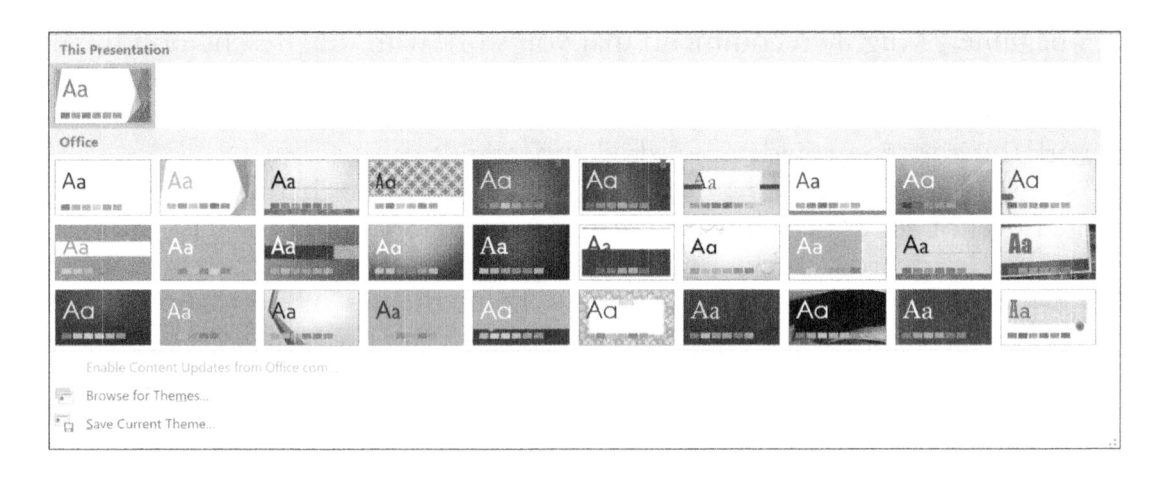

I recommend when choosing a theme that you look at how that theme will appear when applied to both a Title slide as well as a Title and Content slide before making your choice, because they can be very different.

For example, the slide on the next page is from the Integral theme and is very simple. But the title slide for that theme is dominated by a decorative pattern that is not.

Also, theoretically, the text color that will be used in the headers on your presentation is the same one used for the Aa on the thumbnail image but it's good to confirm that by seeing the theme on a slide.

And the colored boxes that run along the bottom of each thumbnail do show the main color palette for the theme, but most themes will only use the first color or two for bullets or effects.

Presentation Themes

For example, here is a slide using the Integral theme and it only uses one accent color:

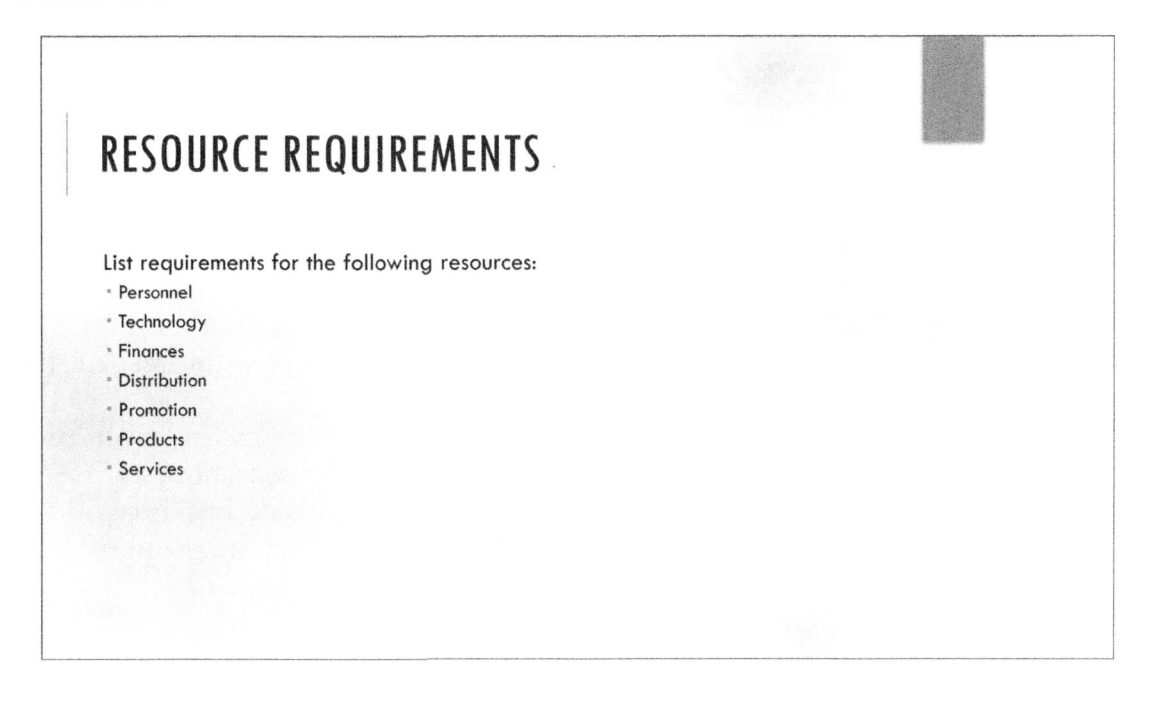

RESOURCE REQUIREMENTS

List requirements for the following resources:
- Personnel
- Technology
- Finances
- Distribution
- Promotion
- Products
- Services

If you add charts, etc. you will see more of the theme colors used and they are all available for any text, element, etc. color choice that you make.

So always a good idea to preview your themes. And to do so on both a title slide and a content slide. (If you don't already have a content slide, right-click in the left-hand task pane and choose New Slide.)

Once you've found a theme you like, to permanently apply it to your slides, simply click on it.

That should apply the theme to every slide in your entire presentation. But it won't do so if you'd selected a subset of your slides before choosing the theme. It also may not do so if your presentation has sections in it.

(Which is why it's always good to start with the right theme so that you don't have to worry about these issues later.)

In addition to the choices you can see in the Themes section of the Design tab, some themes also have what are called variants. Variants use the same structure and design elements but have different color palettes or use different background colors or patterns.

Not every theme has a variant, but when a theme does have variants you will see them in the Variants section of the Design tab.

They only appear after you have selected that specific theme. Here, for example, is the variant section for the Integral theme.

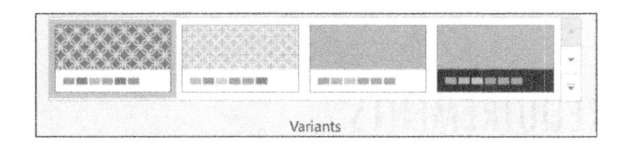

The first thumbnail is the default option for that theme. The remaining thumbnails show the variants.

Just like with the Themes section if there are more than three variants available you can use the arrows on the right-hand side to see the rest of the choices.

Also, as with the theme thumbnails, you can hold your mouse over each variant to see what it will look like when applied to your presentation.

In this example, at least two of the variants use a non-white background for the main slides in the presentation. A couple also use more than one of the theme colors, so there can definitely be some variety within a theme.

But they all do keep the general design elements the same. Here is an example of one of the variants for the Integral theme:

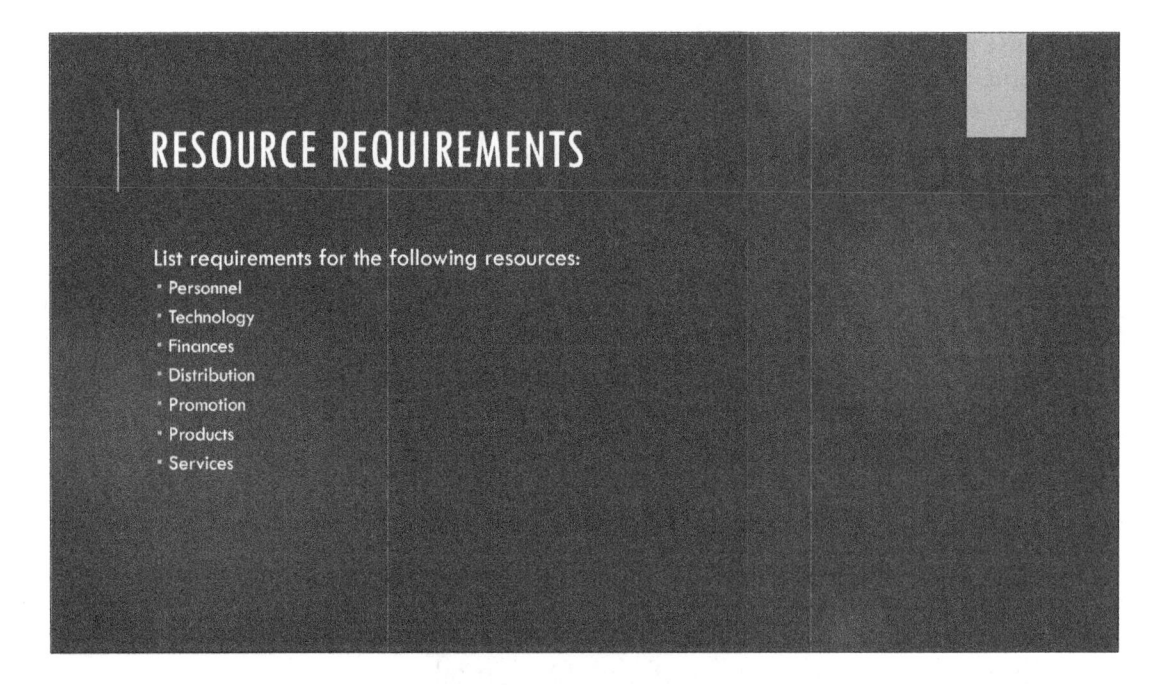

Presentation Themes

Be careful when applying a new theme that all of your existing slides work with that new theme. It is possible for the main slides to work but the title slide to no longer have an acceptable appearance. Or vice versa.

If you find a presentation theme that you like but still can't find colors that work for you amongst the variant thumbnails, you can instead change the colors using the Colors dropdown menu under Variants in the Design tab.

To access it, click on the downward arrow with a line on the right-hand side of the Variants thumbnail display. That will bring up a dropdown menu that includes the Colors option. Hold your mouse over that Colors option and a secondary dropdown menu will appear that shows various color palettes.

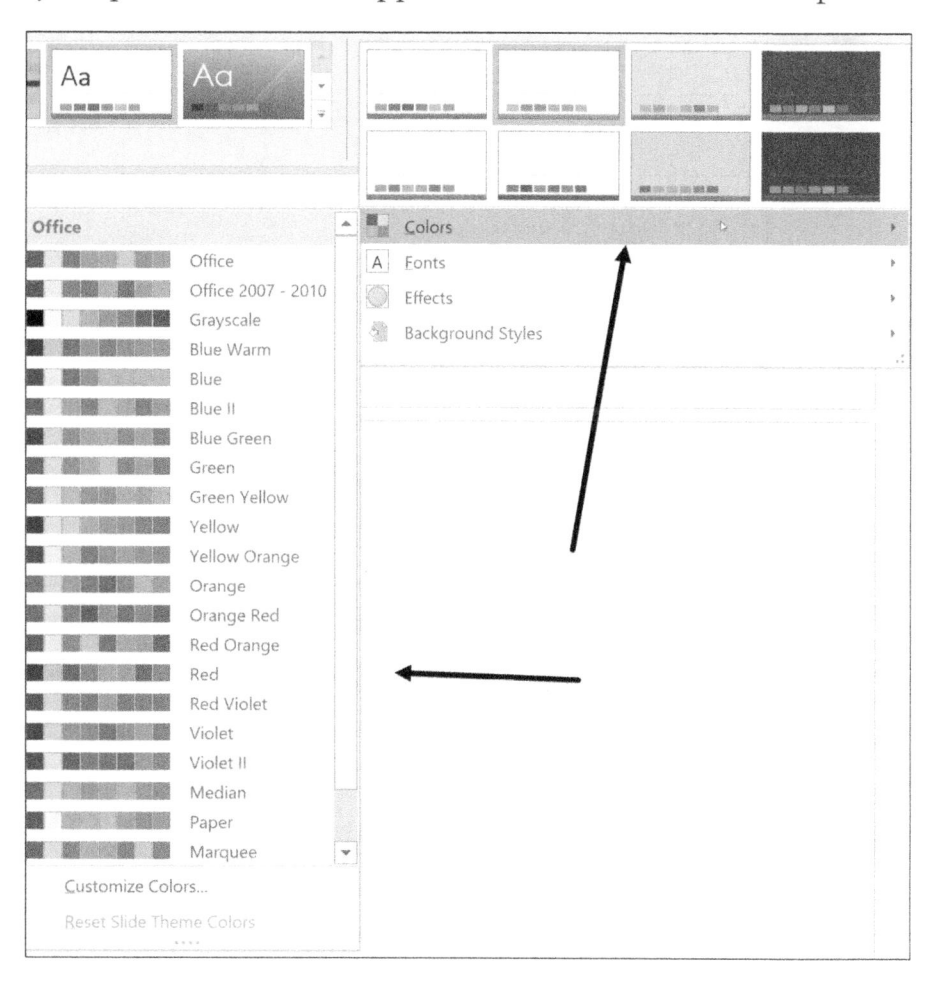

33

Just like with the theme and variant thumbnails, you can hold your mouse over each color palette to see how it will appear in your presentation. Click on one to permanently apply it.

Changing your theme should definitely not be the last thing you do. Ideally you choose a theme before you start to add your content so that you can adjust as you add your content. But in case it's needed, that's how you do it.

Okay, then. Now let's talk about the various slide layouts that may be available as part of each theme.

Slide Layouts

There are a variety of slide layouts available to you in PowerPoint. Probably more than you'll actually need. But I wanted to run through a handful of the most common ones before we go any farther because I'm going to occasionally refer to a slide layout and I want you to know what I'm talking about when I do.

The images below use the Facet theme with a customized color palette applied.

As mentioned above, to add a new slide into your presentation, right-click in the left-hand task pane and choose New Slide from the dropdown menu.

Or you can go to the Insert tab and choose New Slide from the Slides section. If you click on the dropdown arrow, you can then choose your layout before you insert the slide.

To change the layout of a slide you've already added to your presentation, right-click on the slide, go to Layout, and choose a new layout from the secondary dropdown menu.

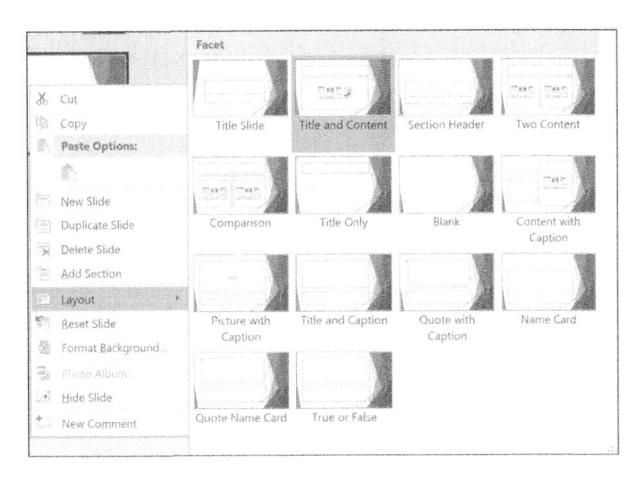

You can also select a slide or slides, go to the Slides section of the Home tab, click on the dropdown arrow next to Layout, and choose your layout from there.

Not all themes or templates will have all layouts. And different themes may have the elements (such as text boxes) of a layout in different locations on the slide. For example, the Slice theme puts the title section of each slide at the bottom of the page instead of the top.

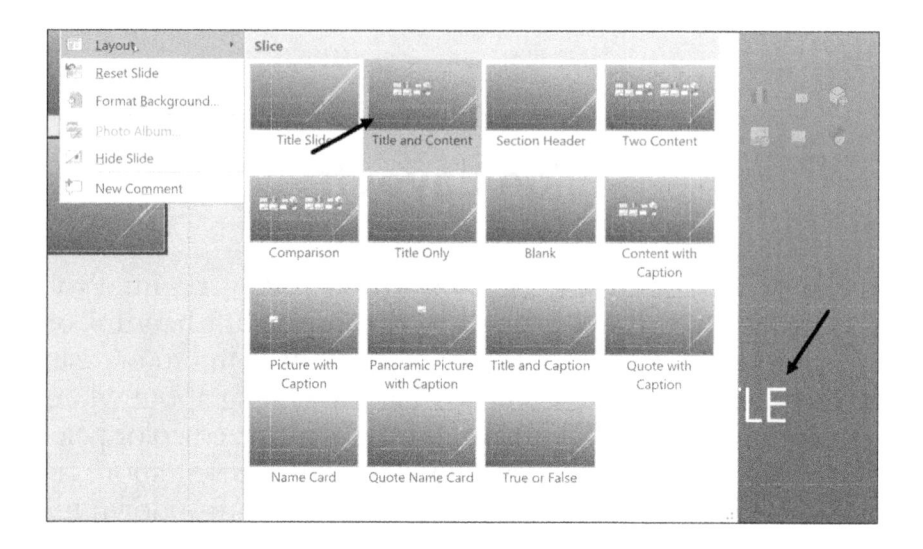

This is why you should definitely look at where the elements are in a presentation theme before you decide to use it.

* * *

Now let's walk through your slide layout choices. In my opinion, you can put together a perfectly adequate presentation with just the Title and Title and Content slides, although there are many more choices than that.

Title Slide

The Title slide is the default first slide for a presentation. It has a section for adding a title and a subtitle and, if you choose one of the templates provided in PowerPoint, a background or design elements that match the chosen theme.

Slide Layouts

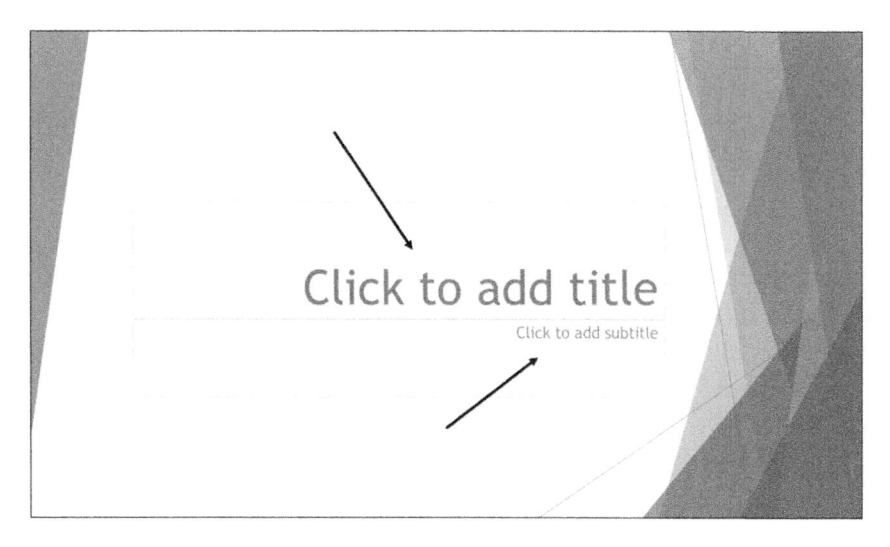

Section Header

If you are going to have sections within your presentation, then you'll want to separate them using a Section Header slide.

This slide has an appearance that is close to that of the title slide, but usually the text or design elements are in a different position. It may also use different colors, fonts, or font colors.

In this theme you can see that the design element on the left-hand side is slightly different from the one used for the title slide. The text is also located in a different location and is a smaller font size.

Title and Content Slide

The Title and Content slide is the one I use for most of my presentations. For a basic presentation with a bulleted set of talking points, this is the slide that you'll probably use the most often.

It has a text box where you can give a high-level title for the slide and then a larger text box that takes up most of the rest of the space on the slide where you can add text or a data table, chart, picture, video, etc.

The design elements on this slide are generally less pronounced than on the title and section slides, but not always.

Here you can see that the design elements are the same as were used on the section slide but that the amount of space for text is much larger and the title is at the top.

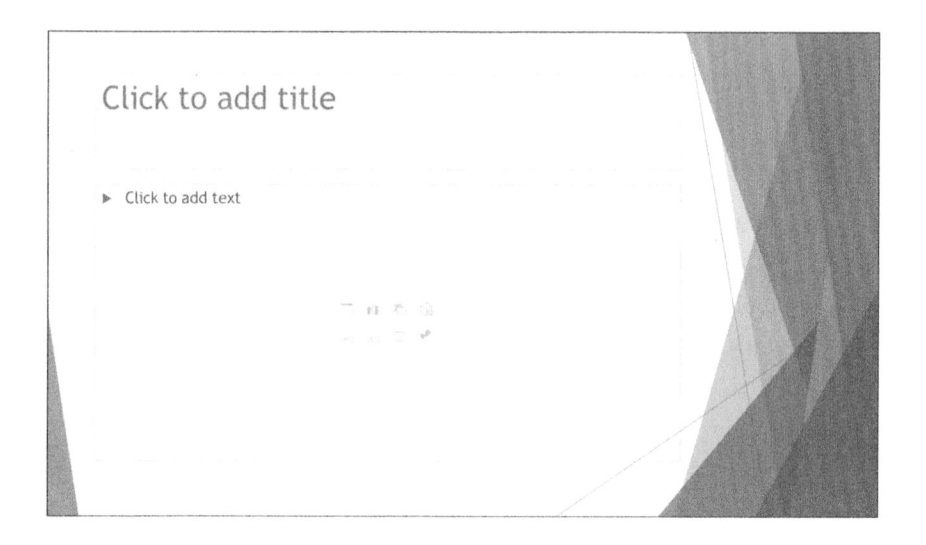

Be careful when moving between themes to check your titles on your slides. Some themes use all caps in the title section and some do not. If you're switching between a theme that uses all caps to one that doesn't, you may find that you need to retype your entries because only half of your words are capitalized the way they should be.

Slide Layouts

Two Content

The Two Content slide is another content slide. This slide has a section for a title and then two separate content boxes. It can be a good choice for when you want to either have two separate bulleted lists side by side or when you want to have text next to an image, data table, video, or chart.

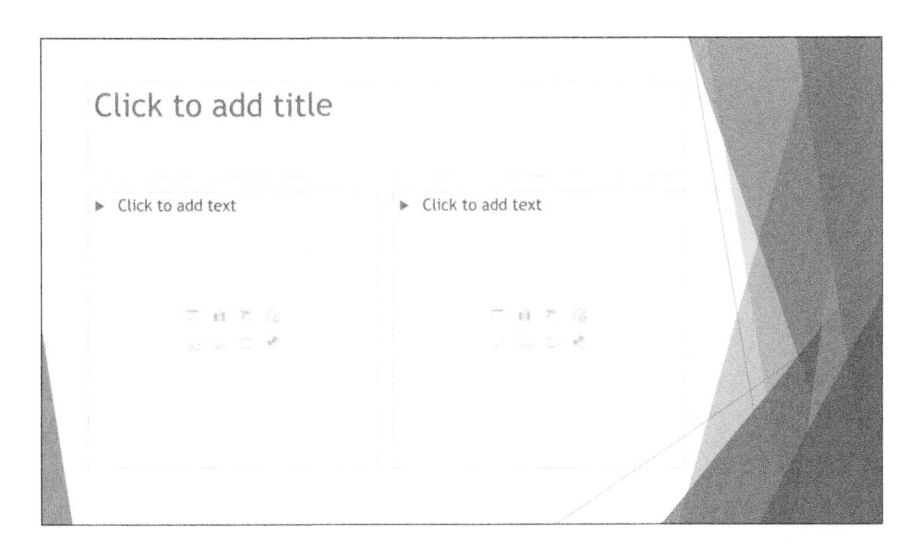

* * *

It can be hard to see the difference between the different slide types when they don't have content in them, so here's a snapshot from the left-hand task pane of the first four slide types we've discussed with content added to them using the Facet theme and then using the Ion Boardroom theme.

The content is exactly the same for both:

M.L. Humphrey

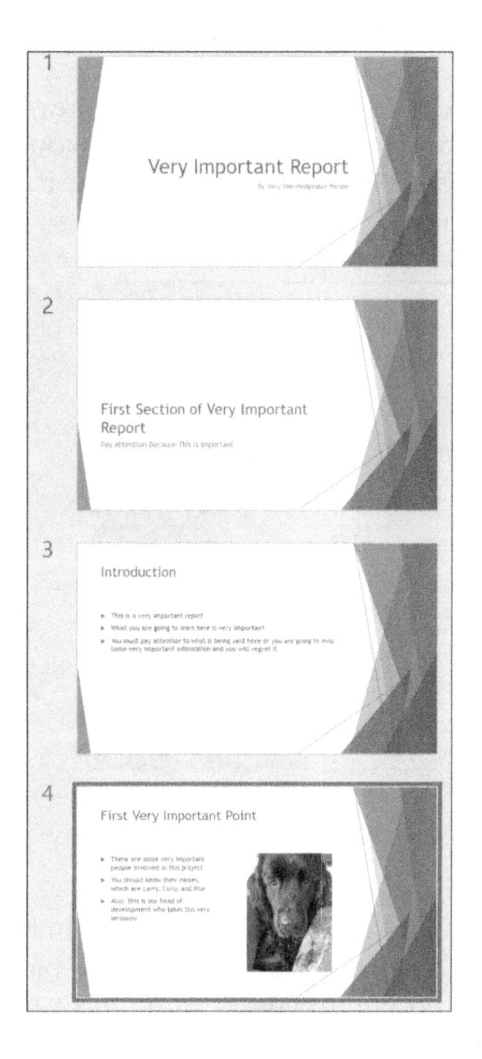

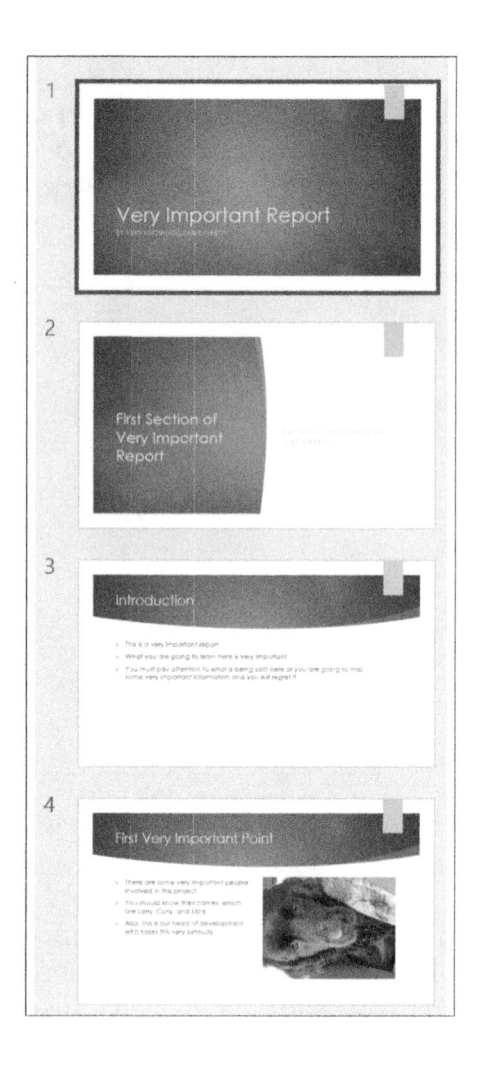

Note that when I changed the theme over to Ion Boardroom it changed the orientation of the image I'd placed on the fourth slide. If you move between themes you need to always go back through your presentation and make sure that all of your text, bullet points, images, etc. still work with the new theme.

* * *

Okay, then. Next slide type.

Comparison

The Comparison slide is a content slide much like the Two Content slide except it has added sections directly above each of the two main text boxes where you can put header text to describe the contents of each of the boxes.

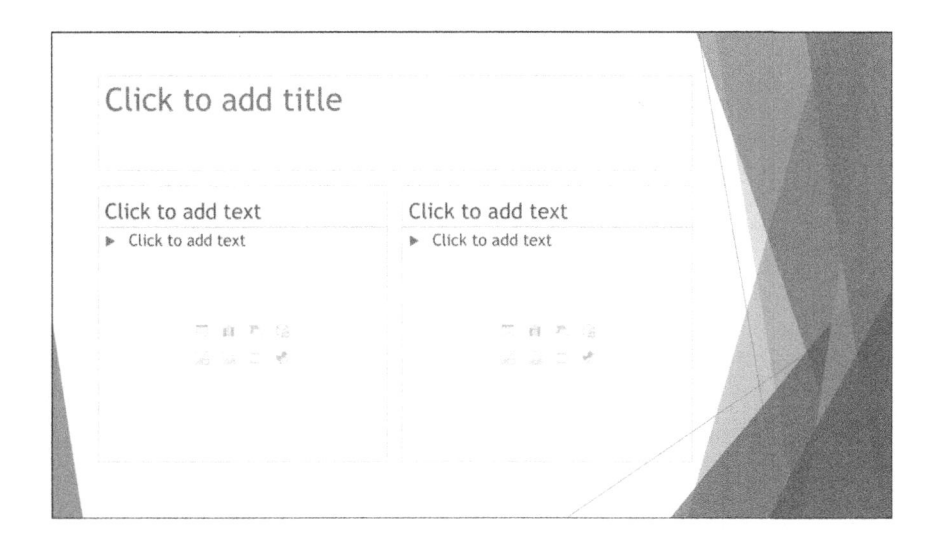

This is especially good for situations where you maybe have side-by-side charts, data tables, videos, or images and you want to be able to label each one.

Title Only

The Title Only slide is a content slide that just has the title section and nothing else. You would generally use this slide when you wanted to add elements to the body of the slide yourself or when you wanted to separate sections and didn't want to use the section header slide.

Blank

The Blank slide has the design elements common to all of the content slides but there are no text boxes on the slide at all.

Content With Caption

The Content With Caption slide is a content slide where the title section covers half of the screen and there are two text boxes where you can add text, images, etc. One of the text boxes is below the title and the other takes up the other half of the slide.

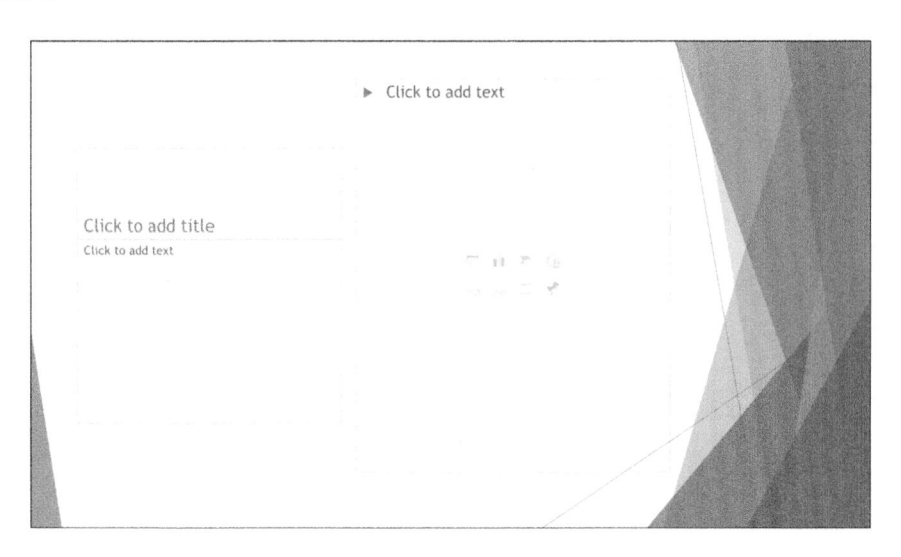

Picture With Caption

The Picture With Caption slide has a large section for a picture and then a text box below it where you can add a title and description of the picture.

Title And Caption

The Title And Caption slide has a large section for a title with a smaller section for text. It would make a good section separator if you wanted a different appearance for a new section such as an Appendix.

Quote With Caption

The Quote With Caption slide is a slide that has quote marks around the main text section and then a smaller text box immediately under that for an attribution of who said the quote. There's also another text box for comments related to the quote.

Slide Layouts

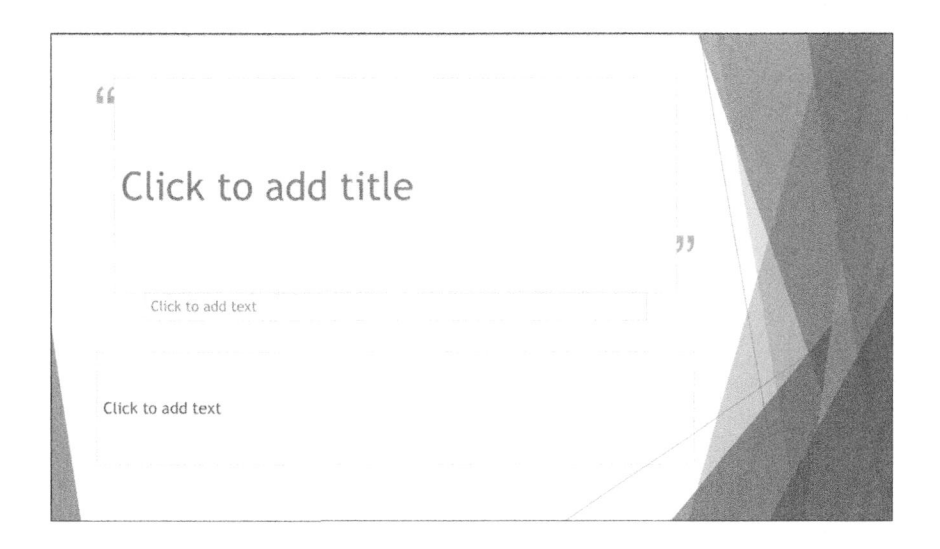

[Slide preview showing "Click to add title" with two "Click to add text" areas]

Other

Some themes will have even more pre-formatted slide types you can use. For example, the Ion Boardroom theme has a three-column slide type and this theme had a Name Card option.

Some themes won't have this many. In that case you can either create what you need by adding on to the Blank or Title Only slides or you can find a theme that better suits your needs.

As I said before, I can put together a perfectly good presentation using the Title and Title and Content slides alone, but it is nice to have more options than that to work with. A presentation where every single slide looks the same can become monotonous and that can lose you the attention of your audience. Although, as always, you need to balance that out against making your presentation more interesting than what you're saying.

Alright, now let's cover how to add content to a slide.

Add and Format Text

Add Text

Adding text to an existing slide is very easy. You simply click and type. For example, here, is a Title slide:

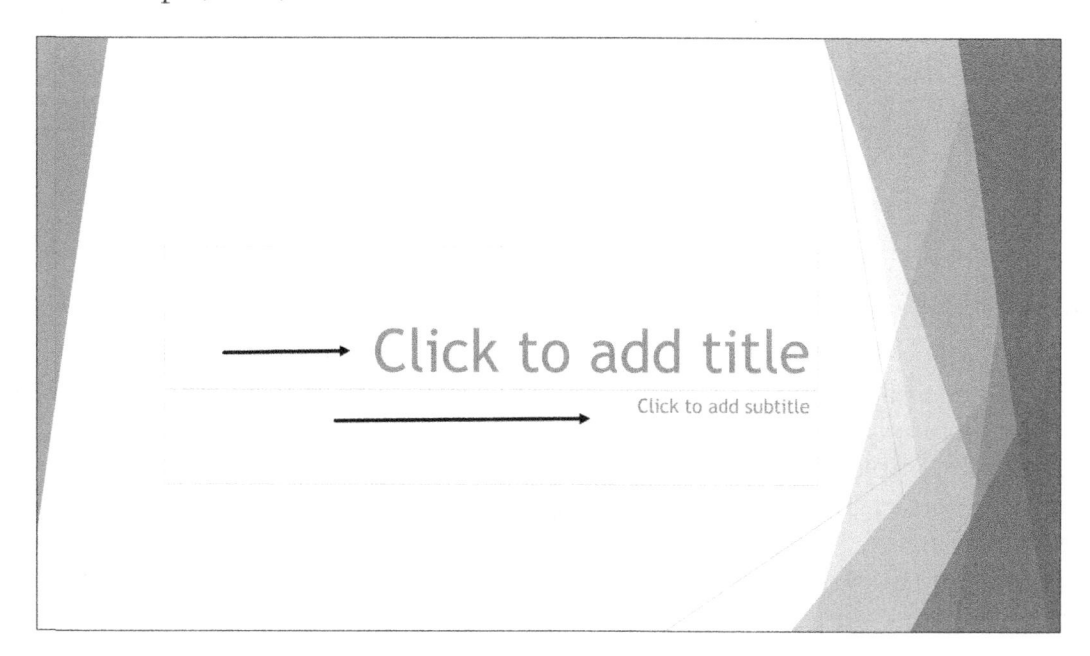

See where it says "Click to add title" and "Click to add subtitle"? Those are both text boxes that are already set up for you to add your text. All you have to do is click on either one and start typing.

When you're done typing in one text box you can click in the other or click elsewhere on the slide.

It works the same for content-style slides. The main Title and Content slide has a text box where it says "Click to add title" and a text box where it says "Click to add text". With this particular theme, the main text is shown as a bulleted list, so you'll see the first bullet is already there and a new bullet will appear each time you hit Enter..

Here is one of those slides completed with three rows of talking points:

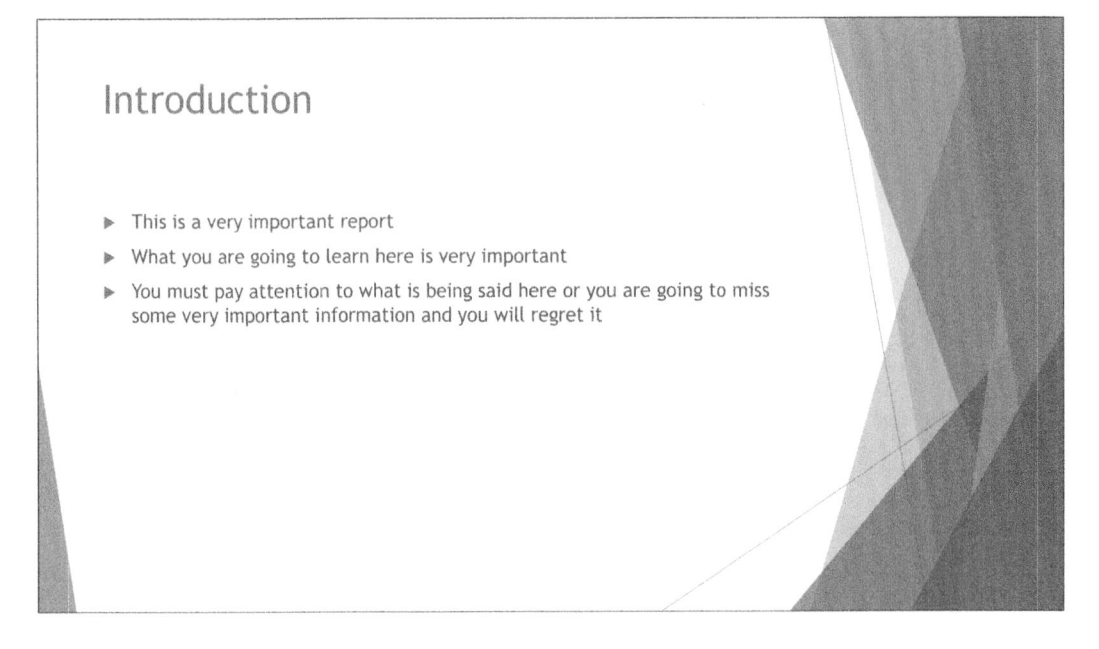

Introduction

▶ This is a very important report
▶ What you are going to learn here is very important
▶ You must pay attention to what is being said here or you are going to miss some very important information and you will regret it

All I had to do was click into the text box and start typing. Each time I hit Enter it started a new line for me that already had a bullet point.

If you need to create subpoints you can use the tab key to indent a line before you start typing your text.

In some templates that will also change the type of bullet used or change the size of the bullet. It will often also change the size of the text. In this next image you can clearly see that the third-level of text is smaller than the first level. In fact, each line goes down by 2 pts in this theme. So the first line is 18 pt, the next is 16 pt, and the third is 14 pt.

Add and Format Text

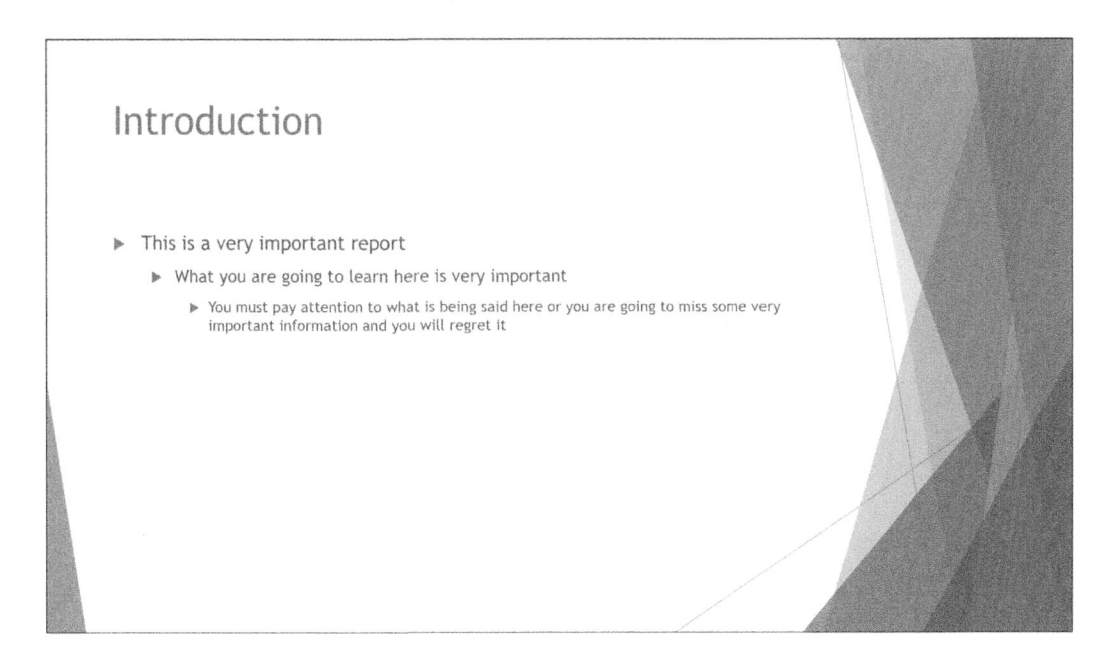

> Introduction
>
> ▸ This is a very important report
>   ▸ What you are going to learn here is very important
>   ▸ You must pay attention to what is being said here or you are going to miss some very important information and you will regret it

To remove an indent, use Shift + Tab before your start typing.

For lines that have already been added where you need to adjust the indent, click to the left of the first letter in that line and then use Tab or Shift + Tab to adjust the indent.

You can also use the Decrease List Level and Increase List Level options in the Paragraph section of the Home tab. They're the ones with lines with an arrow pointing either left or right in the middle of the top row of that section. You can click anywhere on that paragraph to use the option; you don't have to click at the start of the text.

If you want complete control over your indent, you can right-click and choose Paragraph from the dropdown menu. This will bring up the Paragraph dialogue box where you can specify an exact indent amount.

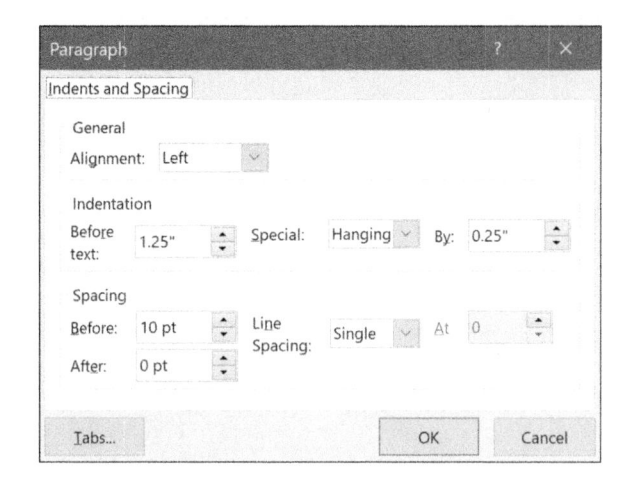

By default the PowerPoint themes use fonts and font sizes that are legible for a presentation given on a projector. That's true for probably the first three levels of indents. But past that point the text may become too small to be legible from a distance.

I wouldn't go below about 14 point for any text on a slide that's meant to be used in a presentation. (As opposed to printed out.) I believe that most of the pre-formatted presentations stop decreasing the font size at 12 point, which may be workable but is just on the edge for me.

Also, sometimes PowerPoint will adjust your text dynamically to make it fit into the text box. So if you use too much text it will make that text smaller than the default in order to get the text to fit.

Because this can happen on a slide-by-slide basis it creates a disjointed presentation when it happens. If one slide has bullet points in a 20 point size and another has bullet points in a 14 point size and another has them in an 11 point size, even if the font and colors are consistent across slides, it can be distracting to a viewer.

Which is why I try when I can to make the font size consistent across slides. The easiest way to do so is to keep your entries short and sweet.

In other words, don't have one slide with a title of "Introduction" and another with a title of "Discussion of the Philosophical Aspects of Polar Ionization and Government Regulatory Structures". Chances are that second slide will automatically be converted to a smaller font size (and may have text that runs outside of the provided text box to boot.)

With bullet points try to keep it to three levels or less. If you can't do that, consider manually adjusting the font size for the fourth-level and beyond bullet points.

Add and Format Text

And if you absolutely can't avoid lengthy text, then adjust the rest of your slides to the size of the lengthiest text entries. For example, with the Facet theme I've been using here, the default title size is 36 point, but when I put in a very lengthy title it is reduced to 32 point. So to create consistency throughout the presentation I'd change any 36 point titles to 32 point.

(Obviously, it's easier to simplify the language instead, but that's not always an option when working on group projects or with a boss who has certain unmovable notions of what should be said.)

Move Text

If you need to cut, copy, or paste text from within a slide, it works much the same way as it did for the slides in the left-hand pane.

To cut text, highlight the text you want to cut and then use Ctrl + X or go to the Clipboard section of the Home tab and choose Cut from there. You can also right-click and choose Cut from the dropdown menu.

As you'll recall, cutting text removes it from its current location but still allows you to paste that text elsewhere.

To copy text, highlight the text you want to copy and then use Ctrl + C or to go to the Clipboard section of the Home tab and choose Copy from there. You can also right-click and choose Copy from the dropdown menu.

Copying keeps the text in its current location but also allows you to paste that text elsewhere.

To paste text, click on the location where you want to place the text you copied or cut and then use Ctrl + V. If you paste text this way it will take on the formatting of the location where you paste it.

Your other options are to click where you want to paste the text and then either go to the Clipboard section of the Home tab and click on the arrow under Paste or right-click and choose one of the paste options from the dropdown menu.

The paste option with the lower case a in the bottom right corner (Use Destination Theme) will use the formatting of the location where you are pasting your text. So font, etc., but it might still keep the font size.

The option with the paintbrush in the bottom right corner (Keep Source Formatting) will keep the formatting the text already had.

The option with the small picture in the bottom right corner (Picture) will paste the selected text in as an image. (You will not be able to edit this text after it's pasted because it will no longer be considered text.)

The option with the large A in the bottom right corner (Keep Text Only), will paste the text into the presentation but use the formatting that would apply to any text you typed into that specific location.

Here I have taken the word Introduction from the title section of a slide and I have pasted it into four separate bullet points that were formatted to use 12 pt Algerian for the font. (So basically a different font, different font size, and different color.)

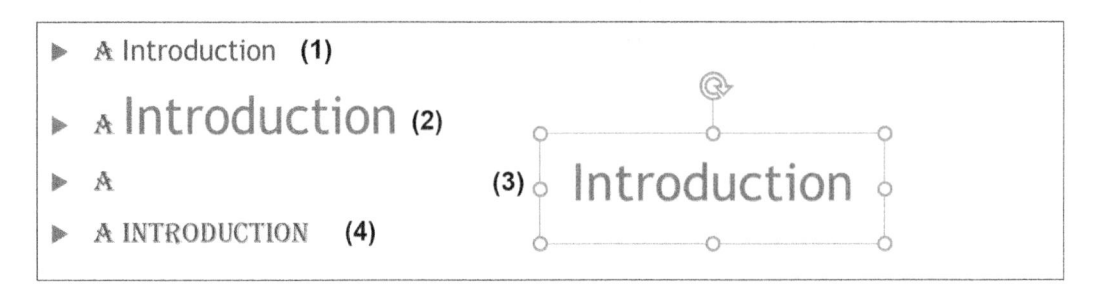

▶ A Introduction **(1)**
▶ A Introduction **(2)**
▶ A   (3) Introduction
▶ A INTRODUCTION **(4)**

You can see that for Use Destination Theme (1) it changed the font size and color but not the font. For Keep Source Formatting (2) nothing changed. For Picture (3) it inserted the text exactly as it existed originally but as a picture. And for Keep Text Only (4) the font, font size, and font color all changed.

Ctrl + V gives the same result as the first line (1), so change of color and size but not font.

Basically, if you're moving text around you may need to do some formatting once it moves unless you remember to Paste – Keep Text Only.

Alright. That's copy/cut and paste. There are more specialized paste options available under the Clipboard option, but for a beginner level I don't think they're worth discussing here. If you want to look at them click on Paste Special from the dropdown to bring up the Paste Special dialogue box.

Delete Text

If you need to remove text you can either cut that text or you can use the Delete or Backspace keys. Backspace will delete text to the left of the cursor. Delete will delete text to the right of the cursor.

If you've highlighted the text you want to delete then either one will work.

Delete and Backspace can also delete bullet points or the numbers or letters in a numbered list.

Change Font Size

To adjust font size, you have a few options.

50

Add and Format Text

First, whichever option you use will require you to make the change before you start typing or to highlight any text you have already typed that you want to change. So do that.

Next, your first option is to go to the Font section of the Home tab and use the font size dropdown to choose a new font size. The current font size should appear in that box unless you've selected text that is more than one size. If that happens, the value will show the smallest font size with a plus sign next to it. So for me just now when I selected four levels of bullet points it showed as 12+ but when I then only selected the top two levels it showed as 16+.

You can either click on the dropdown arrow and select one of the listed font sizes or you can type in your own value.

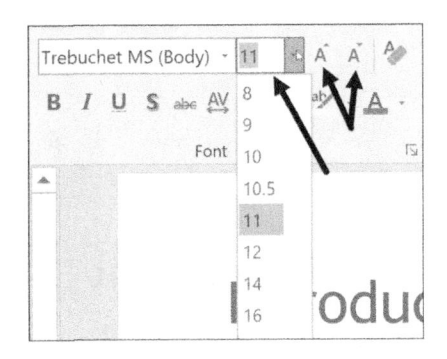

Another way to change the font size is located to the right of the dropdown. There are two capital A's with an arrow in the top right corner. One is to increase font size and the other is to decrease font size. Using those options will increase the font size or decrease it by one spot on the dropdown menu.

So if you have a 10 point font and use the increase font size option it will go up to 10.5 because that's the next available font size in the dropdown. But if you're at 14 it will take you to 16 and 36 will go to 40.

Another option you have is to right-click in the main workspace and use what I refer to as the mini formatting menu. It appears either directly above or directly below the dropdown menu and is a miniature version of the Font section of the Home tab. It has both the font size dropdown menu as well as the increase and decrease font options.

Finally, you can right-click in the main workspace and choose Font from the dropdown menu. This will bring up the Font dialogue box which has a Size option. You can either type in the value you want or use the up and down arrows to change the font size. The size will change by .1 with each use of the up or down arrows. So 14 will go to 14.1, for example.

51

Which means it'll generally be easier to just type in the value you want.

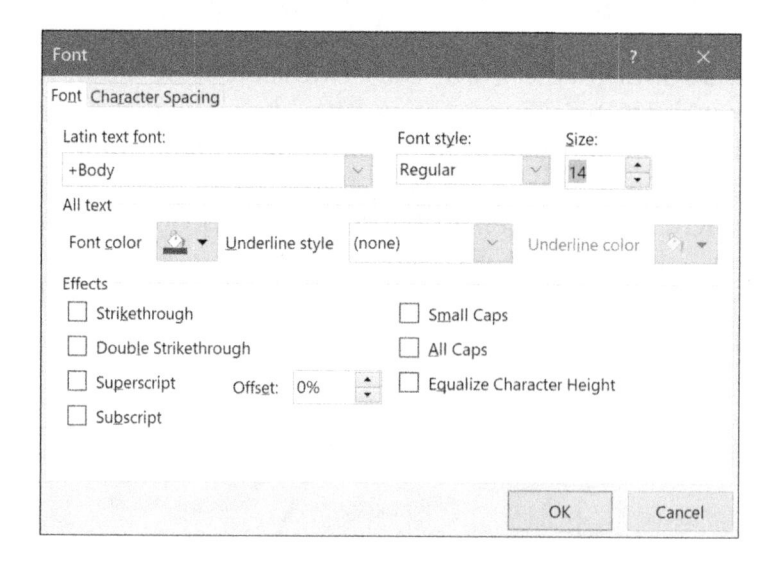

Change Font

In general I wouldn't recommend changing the font because the templates are built to work well with their assigned fonts. But it does sometimes need to be done. For example, a number of my corporate consulting clients have had fonts that they wanted used for all communications to create consistent branding.

As before, you either need to change the font choice before you start typing or you need to select the text you want to change.

Once you've done that, you have a few options for changing your font.

The first is in the Font section of the Home tab. There is a font dropdown menu which is to the left of the font size dropdown menu. In this example the font that's currently in use is Trebuchet MS. To change that font, click on the arrow for the dropdown menu and then click on the font you'd like to use.

Add and Format Text

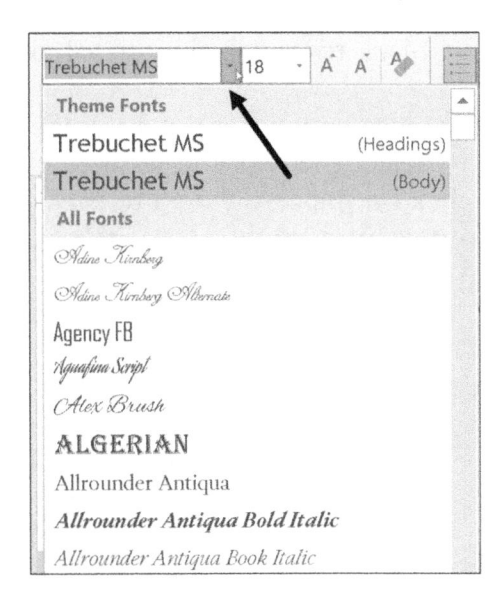

The name of each font in the dropdown menu is written in that font which should help give you an idea of which font to use. I would caution you against using a script (like Aquafina) or a stylized font (like Algerian) for the main text in a presentation slide. A presentation should be about conveying information and the text you use to do that shouldn't get in the way of your communication. Using an overly-ornate font distracts from the text and also from the speaker because your audience is too busy trying to read your slides instead of listen to you.

If you already know the font you want, you can click into the field that shows the current font and start typing the name of the font you'd like. As you type, PowerPoint will auto-complete the field. If you click on the dropdown arrow first and then click into that field and start typing the dropdown list of fonts will move to that part of the alphabet, which comes in handy when the font you want is later in the alphabet.

The mini formatting menu is another available option and works the same way as the Font section of the Home tab.

Or you can right-click and choose Font from the dropdown menu and then change the font choice in the Latin Text Font dropdown menu.

Change Font Color

Another adjustment you might need to make to your text is to change the color of the text. For example, when we discussed the Paste options above some of the options kept the original text color when what would've looked best is changing the font color to black to match the rest of the text in the main body of the slide.

As with all other font choices you either need to make this change before you start typing or you need to select the text you want to change.

Once you've done so click on the arrow next to the A that by default has a red underline in either the Font section of the Home tab or the mini formatting bar.

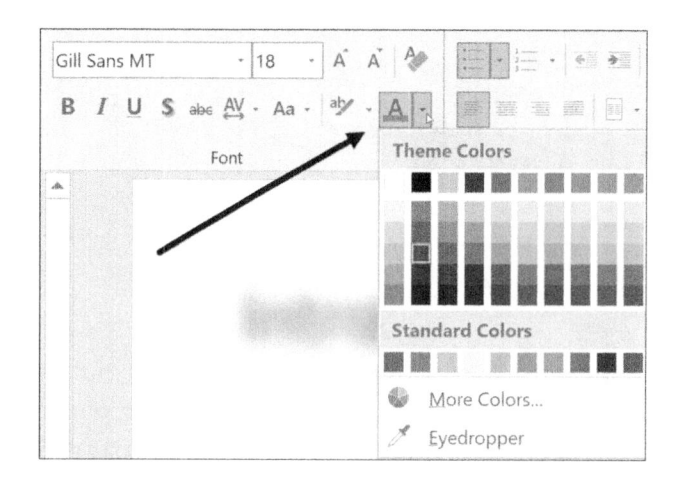

(That line may not always be red. It changes as you change your font color. So the first time you use it, the underline color will change to whatever the last color you used was. This can be useful because then you can just click on the A and apply that color again instead of having to use the dropdown menu each time.)

That initial dropdown menu allows you to choose from one of seventy available colors. Just click on the square for the color you want to use. If you're not sure how a color will look in your presentation, you can hold your mouse over it and your selected text will change to show the color. To apply it, though, you need to click on it.

The Theme Colors section will actually change what colors are shown to you based upon which theme and theme color palette you've chosen. Remember those six colors I mentioned at the bottom of each theme that don't seem to actually get used much? This is where you can find them and apply them yourself as well as shades of each color.

The Standard Colors will not change, however. And if you need a different or a custom color, you can click on the More Colors option which brings up the Colors dialogue box. Within that dialogue box, on the Standard tab you can choose from the honeycomb of colors available by clicking on any of the colored tiles. Or on the Custom tab you can input your own RGB or HSL values.

You can also click into the rainbow of colors above that to select a color or move the black and white slider for different shades of the current color.

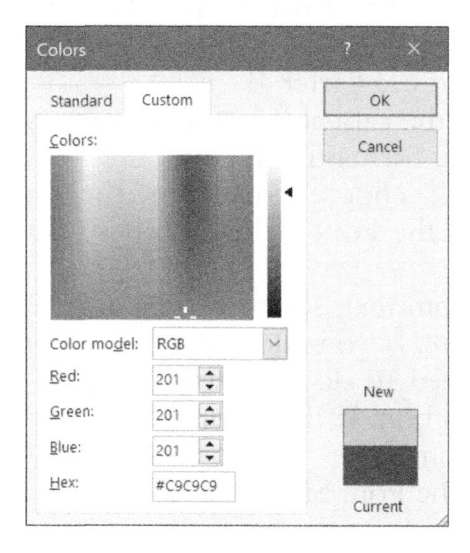

For either the Custom or Standard tab, the color you've selected will show under New in the bottom right corner of the Colors dialogue box and the color you were using previously will show under Current so you can compare them.

When I have corporate clients who have a specified color palette being able to apply the exact right shade of a color using the RGB values is incredibly helpful.

Another option available to you in PowerPoint is the eyedropper. This is for when you already have that color somewhere in your presentation and need to grab it for use elsewhere. For example, I've brought in a cover from a book into a PowerPoint slide so that I could grab the color I need from that cover so that my presentation is consistent with the book it's about.

To use the eyedropper click on the dropdown arrow for Font Color and then choose Eyedropper from the bottom of the dropdown menu. Next, click on the color you want to use from within your presentation. This will change any selected text to that color and will also add the color as a choice under Recent Colors in the Font Color dropdown menu.

Another option for changing your font color is to right-click on your presentation slide and choose Font from the dropdown menu to open the Font dialogue box. On the Font tab you can then click on the dropdown arrow for the Font Color option. It's identical to the other two choices except that it won't have the eyedropper option.

Bold Text

To bold text either select the text you want to bold or make your choice before you start typing.

The easiest option is to use Ctrl + B.

You can also click on the capital B in the bottom row of the Font section of the Home tab or the mini formatting menu.

Or you can right-click, choose Font from the dropdown menu, and then change the Font Style in the Font dialogue box to Bold. Use Bold Italic if you want both bold and italic.

To remove bolding from text, select the text and either click on the capital B or use Ctrl + B once more. If you select text that is partially bolded and partially not bolded, you may need to do this twice because the first time may apply bolding to the entire selection. If that happens then the second time will remove it from the entire selection.

You can also change the Font Style back to Regular in the Font dialogue box.

Italicize Text

To italicize text either select the text you want to italicize or make your choice before you start typing.

The easiest option is to use Ctrl + I.

You can also click on the slanted capital I in the bottom row of the Font section of the Home tab or the mini formatting menu.

Or you can right-click, choose Font from the dropdown menu, and then change the Font Style in the Font dialogue box to Italic. As above, use Bold Italic if you want both bold and italic.

To remove italics from text, select the text and either click on the slanted capital I or use Ctrl + I once more. If you select text that is partially italicized and partially not, you may need to do this twice.

You can also change the Font Style back to Regular in the Font dialogue box.

Underline Text

To underline text either select the text you want to underline or make your choice before you start typing.

Add and Format Text

The easiest option is to use Ctrl + U. This will place a single underline under your text.

You can also click on the underlined U in the bottom row of the Font section of the Home tab or the mini formatting menu.

If you want a wider variety of choices for how to underline your text, right-click and choose Font from the dropdown menu. You can then click on the arrow for the Underline Style dropdown and choose from a variety of underline styles including a double underline, a darker underline, as well as dashed, dotted, and wavy lines.

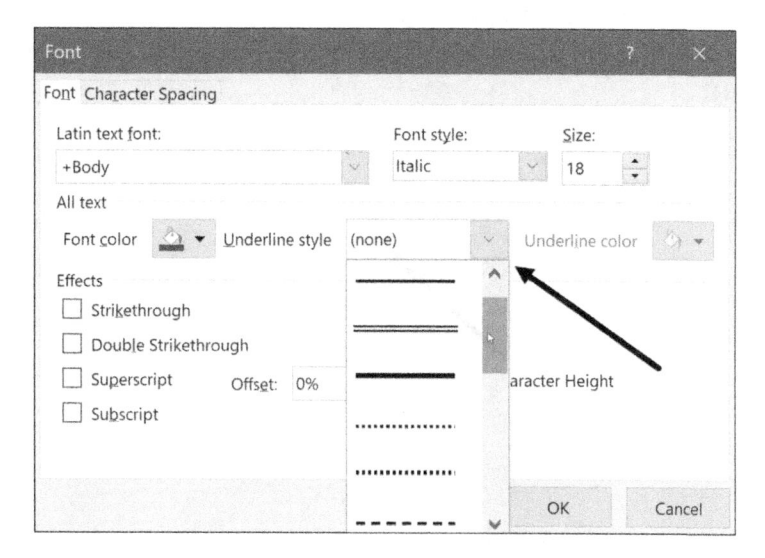

To remove underlining from text, select the text and either click on the capital U with a line under it or use Ctrl + U once more. If you select text that is partially underlined and partially not, you may need to do this twice. If the type of underline was a specialized underline and not the basic single-line style, you will also need to do this twice because the first time you use Ctrl + U or click on the U in the Font section it will convert the specialized underline to a standard single-line underline.

You can also go to the Font dialogue box and change the Underline Style to none, which is the first option.

Change Case

If you want your text to be in all caps or if you have text that is already in all caps that you want to change to normal case, then you will need to change the case of that text.

For this one you have to type the text first and then select it and make the change.

The change case option shows as a capital A followed by a lower-case a, so Aa, and is located in the bottom row of the Font section of the Home tab. It is not an option in the mini formatting menu.

Click on the dropdown arrow to see your available choices and then click on the one you want.

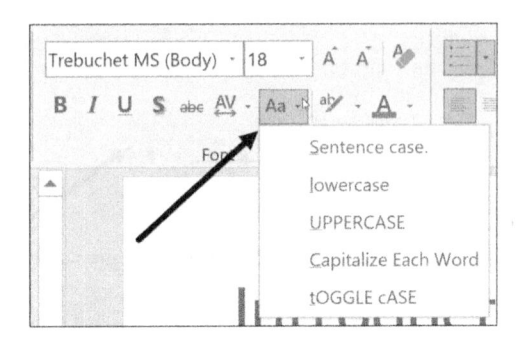

Each choice is written in that style. You can choose between sentence case, lower case, upper case, capitalize each word, and toggle case. (For a presentation unless you have a very good reason for doing so, do not use toggle case.)

Sentence case will capitalize the first letter of the first word in each sentence or text string.

Lower case will put all of the letters in lower case.

Upper case will put all of the letters in upper case.

Capitalize each word will capitalize the first letter of each word.

Toggle case will put the first letter of each word in lower case and all other letters in upper case.

Another option you have is to right-click and choose Font from the dropdown menu but that will only let you apply the upper case option. (By checking the box for all caps).

It does, however, also include an option for small caps which sometimes looks better than using upper case. See here for an example:

> ALL CAPS
> SMALL CAPS

Clear Text Formatting

If you've edited a text selection and want to return it to the default for that theme, you can select the text and then click on the small A with an eraser in the top right corner of the Font section. (If you hold your mouse over it, it will show as Clear All Formatting.)

This will change the selection to whatever font, font size, and font formatting would be appropriate for that location within that theme. It does not change the case of the letters if you used the dropdown menu in the Font section, but it will revert the font, font color, font size, and any bold, italics or underline back to the default for the theme.

Other

You'll note that there were a few other options available in the Font section of the Home tab (text shadowing, strikethrough, and character spacing) as well as additional options in the Font dialogue box.

I've chosen not to cover them here because I want to keep this guide focused on a basic level of PowerPoint presentation and those are ones I expect you wouldn't use as often.

But if there's a text effect you want to apply in a PowerPoint slide that I didn't cover, the Font section of the Home tab or right-clicking and choosing Font to bring up the Font dialogue box are generally where you'll find them.

For more advanced text formatting look to the Drawing Tools Format tab which will appear when you click on any text box in your presentation. There you can apply WordArt styles, text fills, text outlines, and text effects.

Okay. Now let's talk about paragraph-level formatting.

Format Paragraphs

What we just talked about are formatting changes that you can make at the level of an individual word. But there are other changes you can make at the paragraph level. These are generally available through the Paragraph section of the Home tab but some of them are also available in the mini formatting menu or by right-clicking and choosing Paragraph from the dropdown menu.

With the paragraph formatting options you don't have to highlight all of the text you want to change, you just need to be clicked somewhere into the paragraph or section you want to change.

Let's start with one we already covered earlier, Decrease List Level and Increase List Level.

Decrease List Level/Increase List Level

A lot of PowerPoint presentations rely on using bulleted lists. And when you use a bulleted list you will often want to either indent the next line or decrease the indent of the next line.

To indent the next line, you can either click at the beginning of the line and use the Tab key, or you can click anywhere on the line and use the Increase List Level option in the Paragraph section of the Home tab. It's the one that has an arrow pointing to the right at a series of lines.

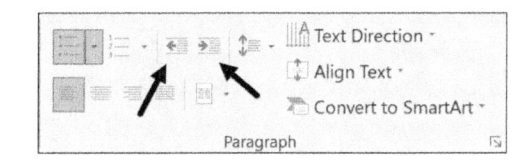

To decrease the indent on a line you can either click at the beginning of the line and use Shift + Tab (so hold down the Shift key and the Tab key at the same time) or you can click anywhere on the line and use the Decease List Level option in the Paragraph section of the Home tab. This is the one with a left-pointing arrow embedded in a series of lines.

If either option is grayed out that's because you can't increase or decrease that indent any further.

These options may or may not be available with plain text that isn't already bulleted or numbered. It will depend on where the text is located within the presentation slide. For example, you generally won't have an indent option in the title section of a slide.

If you have to use very specific placement for your text, you can also right-click and choose Paragraph from the dropdown menu and then use the Paragraph dialogue box to set your indent. It's the value for Before Text in the Indentation section.

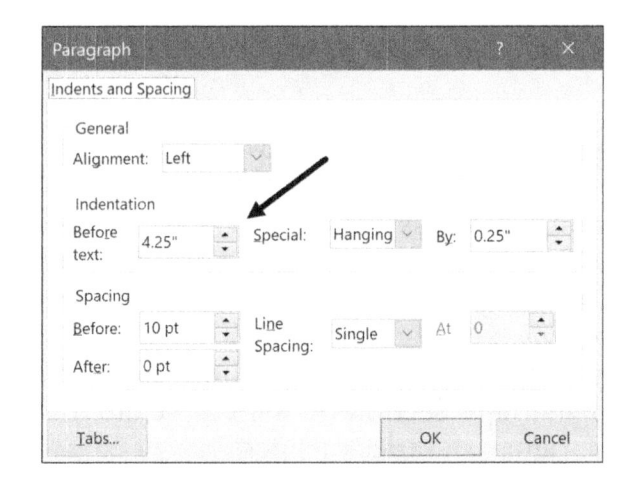

Format Paragraphs

Hanging Indent

Next let's talk about setting a hanging indent or removing one since that's a visible option there in the Paragraph dialogue box and it can be useful to know. (Although keep in mind that if you're working with one of the pre-formatted themes it will likely already have these settings applied and the less you mess with them the better.)

A hanging indent has to do with where your lines of text will start when you have more than one line of text. This is generally used for bulleted and numbered items.

Here is an example where the paragraph is set to have a hanging indent so that the text on all of the lines starts at the same spot. See how the words "also", "development", and "seriously" line up?

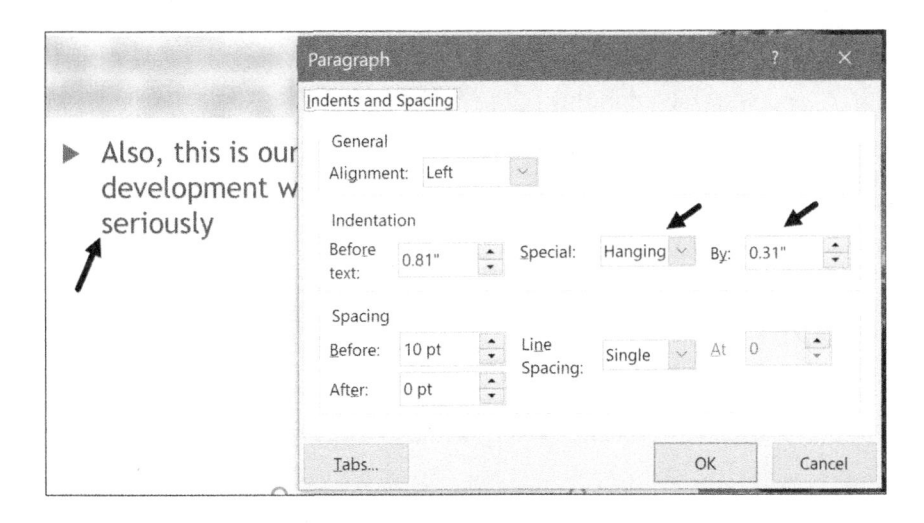

The amount of the indent required to make that happen will be driven by the font and font size. Also by the value you have for "before text".

For each bulleted level on this page the values in the "before text" and "by" fields is different. (This is why it's best not to mess with this and just let PowerPoint do all of it for you.)

If you remove a hanging indent for a bulleted item, it will look like this:

63

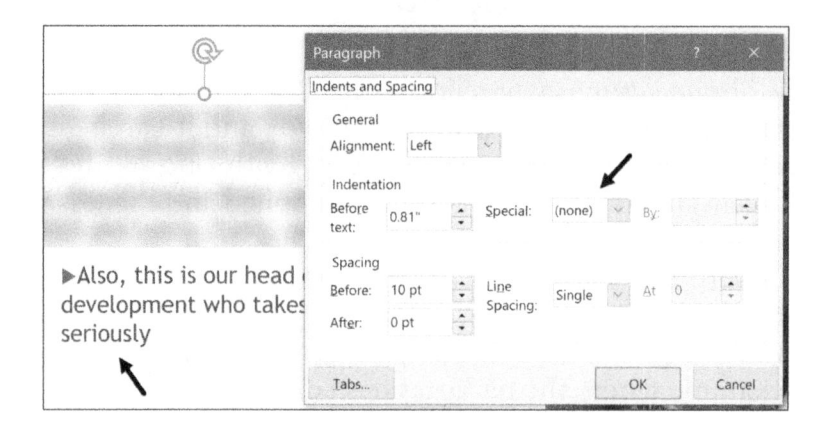

And if you change it to have a first line indent (depending on the value you use), it will look like this:

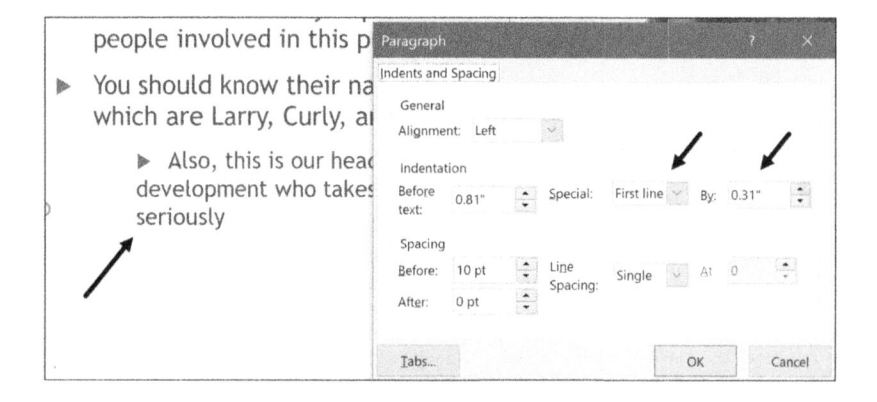

As I said before, I'd generally leave these settings alone, but I have had at least one employer who hadn't created a template for their staff to use, but insisted on very specific indenting for each bulleted item, and the only way to get what they wanted was to adjust these indentation settings.

Okay, then. On to paragraph alignment.

Paragraph Alignment

Your next option is to change the alignment of the text in your paragraph. You have four options.

You can have left-aligned text, meaning that the lines in your paragraph are aligned along the left-hand side.

Format Paragraphs

You can have centered text, meaning each line is aligned along the center.

You can have right-aligned text, meaning each line is aligned along the right-hand side.

Or you can have justified text meaning your text will be spread out across the text box so that it's aligned along both the left- and right-hand side.

Here are examples using the same text where I've copied and pasted it four times and only changed the alignment and the descriptor (left-aligned, centered, etc.)

> - This is to show you what **left-aligned** text looks like. We need enough text for you to really see how it works.
>
> - This is to show you what **centered** text looks like. We need enough text for you to really see how it works.
>
> - This is to show you what **right-aligned** text looks like. We need enough text for you to really see how it works.
>
> - This is to show you what **justified** text looks like. We need enough text for you to really see how it works.

For bulleted points in the main body of the presentation you can see that left-aligned is generally going to be the choice you want, although justified can work as well. Centered is usually best for headers or titles.

To change the alignment of a paragraph, you can go to the Paragraph section of the Home tab and click on one of the alignment options in the bottom row. Each one is a series of lines that shows its alignment type. Click on the one you want to apply it.

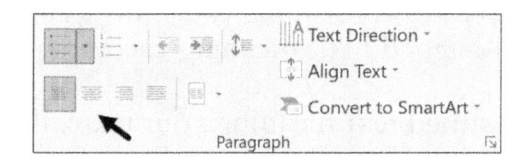

The left, center, and right alignment options are also available in the mini formatting menu.

Or you can right-click, choose Paragraph, and change the alignment using the dropdown menu in the General section. That dropdown has one more option, Distributed which will stretch your line of text across the entire space. I generally don't recommend that for a normal paragraph because the last line won't look good.

Depending on where your text is and what type of text box it is, your selected alignment will either apply to just that paragraph or to all of the contents of the text box. So if you want to use more than one alignment type on a slide (which I generally wouldn't recommend) you may need to use more than one text box to make that happen.

Text Alignment

In addition to setting your paragraph alignment you can also set how the text in a text box will align itself with respect to that text box. Your choices are top, middle, or bottom. Here are examples of each. I've clicked into the middle text box so you can see the outlines of the box. All three paragraphs are in identical text boxes that I've just copied and pasted side-by-side and then changed the alignment to top, middle, and bottom.

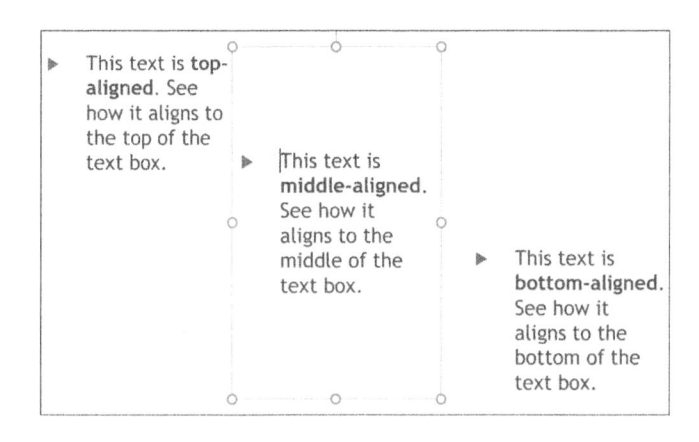

Format Paragraphs

To choose which alignment option you want, go to the Paragraph section of the Home tab and click on the arrow next to Align Text on the right-hand side of the section. This will give you a dropdown menu where you can then click on either Top, Middle, or Bottom.

Your choice will apply to all text within that text box.

If you click on More Options that will open a Format Shape task pane where you can also choose to center the text at the same time.

Using Multiple Columns

If you want your text displayed on a slide in multiple columns you have two choices.

First, you can choose a slide layout that has two equally sized sections like the Two Content slide format and then input your text into both of those boxes, split evenly across the two boxes.

Or, you can use the multiple column formatting option. To split text into multiple columns, simply click anywhere within that text and then go to the Paragraph section of the Home tab and click on the arrow next to the Add or Remove Columns option. (This is the one in the center of the bottom row of that section that shows two sets of lines side by side with a dropdown arrow on the right-hand side.) It is directly to the right of the left, center, right, and justify paragraph options.

You can choose between One Column, Two Columns, Three Columns, or More Columns.

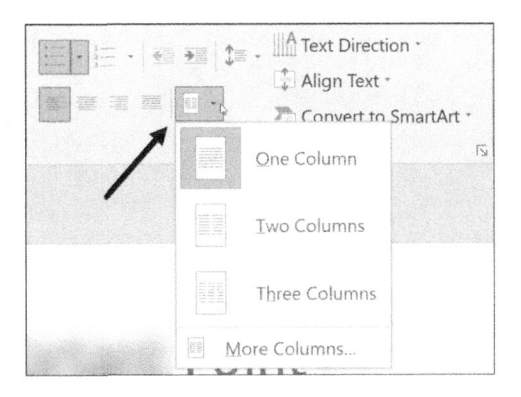

If you click on More Columns you can specify not only the number of columns, but the spacing between them.

The way multiple columns work is that PowerPoint will fill the first column completely before it moves on to putting text into the second column. It does

67

not try to balance across your columns, nor does it make an effort to break a column at a bulleted or numbered point.

Since PowerPoint does not have column breaks like Word does, if you want a specific line to start your second column you have to manually make that happen by using Enter to move that line down far enough that it will move over to the second column.

Also, when you add multiple columns they will appear within that designated text box which can sometimes not look great if the text box is too narrow to really support multiple columns.

In some respects adding multiple text boxes to your slide is a better way to have the appearance of multiple columns while being able to better control the appearance of the text on your slide.

Change Spacing Between Lines of Text

If you want to change the amount of space that appears between lines of text, you can do so by clicking into the paragraph you want to change and then going to the Paragraph section of the Home tab and clicking on the arrow next to the Line Spacing option which is in the top row to the right of the increase list level option. It has arrows pointing upward and downward next to a set of lines.

Click on the dropdown arrow to see the available options. As you hold your mouse over each one you'll see what it looks like in the presentation itself. Click on one to select it.

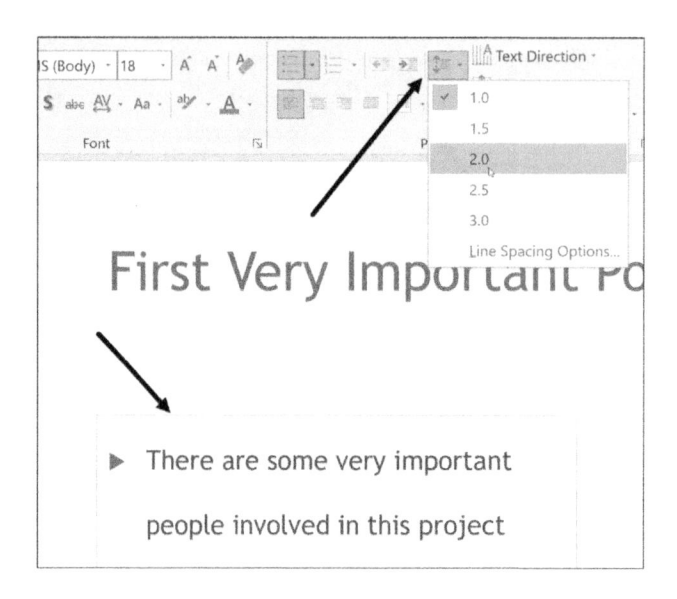

Format Paragraphs

If you choose Line Spacing Options that will bring up the Paragraph dialogue box which can also be opened by right-clicking in the main workspace and choosing Paragraph from the dropdown menu there.

The line spacing options are available in a dropdown in the Spacing section of the dialogue box. In that section of the Paragraph dialogue box you can also change the values for Before and After to place space between your paragraphs.

Here, for example, I've changed the After value to 18 to place a large space between each of these items:

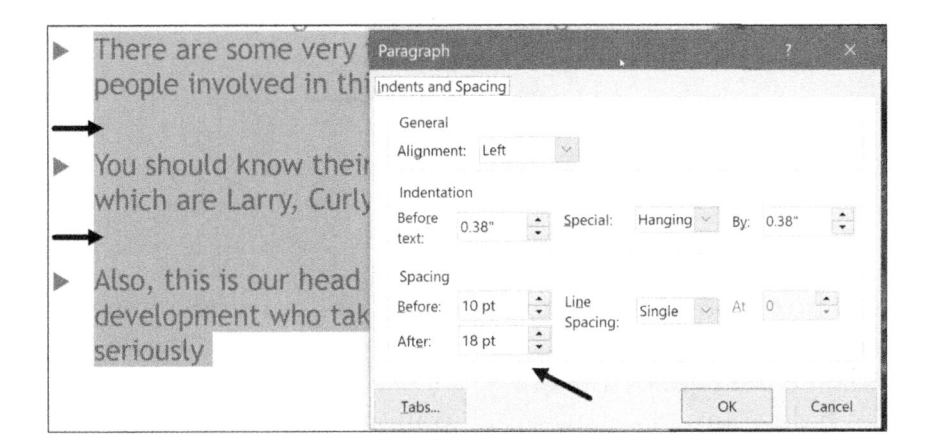

Bulleted Lists

By default, most of the templates include bullets within the main body of each presentation slide. If you want to change the type of bullet, turn off bullets for a specific line, add a bullet to a specific line, or change the bullets to numbers, then you can do so with the Bullets and Numbering options in the top left corner of the Paragraph section of the Home tab.

To change the type of bullet, click on the row you want to change or highlight all of your rows if there's more than one, and then go to the Bullets option (the one with dots next to lines in the top left corner of the Paragraph section of the Home tab) and click on the dropdown arrow.

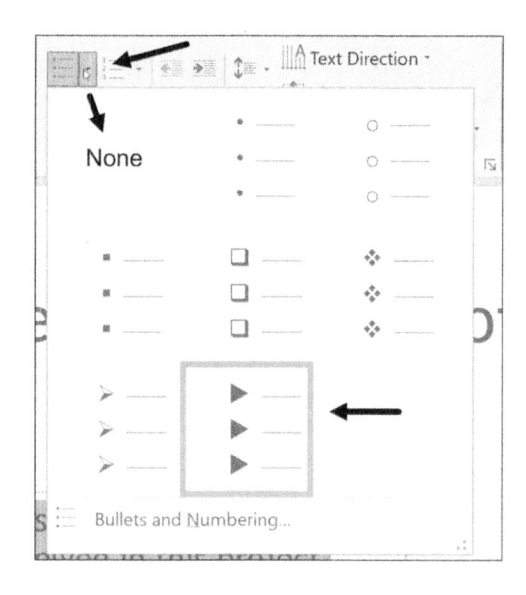

You'll see a box around the type of bullet that's currently being used. Click on None if you don't want a bulleted list. Click on one of the other options if you want to change the type of bullet.

You can hold your cursor over each option to see what it will look like before you make your selection.

Clicking on Bullets and Numbering at the bottom of that list will let you specify the size of the bullet relative to the text as well as the color of the bullet.

If you click on Customize that will let you choose any symbol from the Symbol dialogue box which gives you access to all of the symbols used in fonts like Wingdings which have a number of various shapes available. For example, I was able to change my bullets to a three-leaf clover just now.

The Picture option lets you insert a picture for your bullet.

(But remember that the more you customize things, the more work you have to do throughout your presentation to keep everything uniform and, also, that the you don't want to do something with the formatting of your presentation that distracts from the actual presentation. So, yes, I can in fact make bullets that are pictures of my dog, but that doesn't mean I should.)

Numbered Lists

If you want a numbered or lettered list instead (e.g., 1, 2, 3 or A, B, C) then click on the Numbering dropdown. There you can see a list of available numbered list options to choose from.

Format Paragraphs

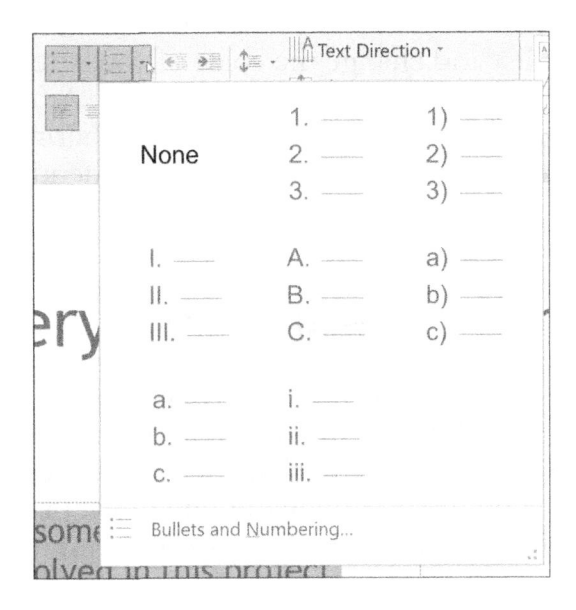

If you need to start at a number other than 1 or a letter other than A, click on Bullets and Numbering at the bottom of the list and then choose your starting point using the Start At box in the bottom right.

For lettered lists (A, B, C) when you change that numeric value for Start At it will change the letter. So a 1 equals A, a 2 equals B, etc.

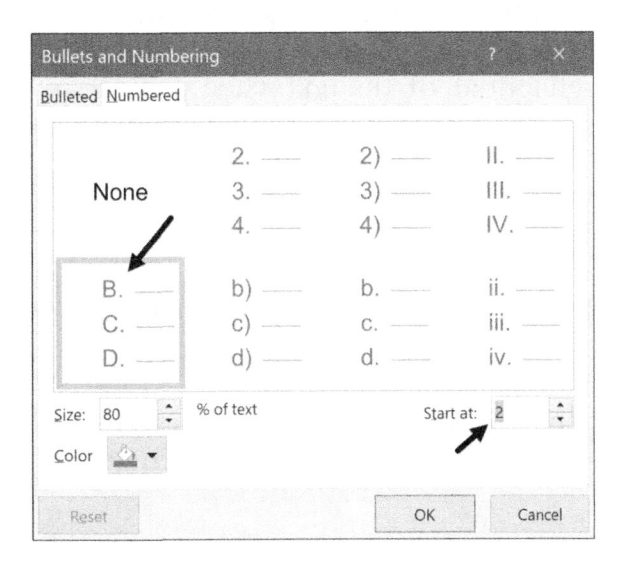

As with the bulleted list, you can also change the relative size of the number or letter compared to the list and change the color of the letter or number using this dialogue box.

Another option for changing both bullets or numbering is to right-click and go to either Bullets or Numbering in the dropdown menu. There is a secondary dropdown that is identical to the one you'll find for each in the Paragraph section of the Home tab.

Format Painter

If you ever find yourself in a situation where the formatting on one section of your presentation or your slide doesn't match another and you don't want to be bothered trying to figure out exactly what the differences are, you can use the Format Painter to copy the formatting from one block of text to another.

This tool can be a lifesaver if someone has done weird things in a presentation you're trying to fix.

To use it, first highlight the text that's formatted the way you want. Next, click on the Format Painter option in the Clipboard section of the Home tab. Then highlight the text that you want to transfer the formatting to.

Font, font size, font color, line spacing, and type of bulleting/numbering should all copy over to the selected text.

You will know that the format painter is on when you see a small paint brush next to your cursor. It will normally turn off the next time you click on text in your presentation, so be sure to go directly to the text you want to transfer the formatting to and highlight all of the text when you do so.

If you have more than one place you want to transfer formatting to, you can double-click on the Format Painter tool and then it will remain on until you turn it back off. To turn it off use the Esc key or click on Format Painter in the Clipboard section of the Home tab once more.

If the result isn't what you wanted or expected use Ctrl + Z to undo it and try again. Sometimes with paragraphs of text it can matter whether you selected the initial paragraph from the top or from the bottom. Same with the paragraph you're transferring the formatting to.

Also, if I want spacing between paragraphs to transfer I always try to select more than one paragraph before I click on the Format Painter.

Add Other Items To a Presentation Slide

Now that we've covered how to add and format text in your presentation let's discuss what other options you have.

If you look at a blank content slide that hasn't had any text added to it yet, you'll see in the center of the text box that there's usually a series of faded images. For example, this is from a text box in a Two Content slide:

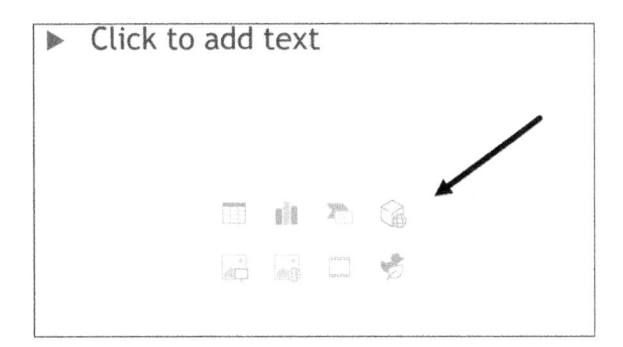

▶ Click to add text

These are the options you have other than just typing text into that box. Your options are Insert Table, Insert Chart, Insert a SmartArt Graphic, 3D Models, Pictures, Online Pictures, Insert Video, and Insert an Icon.

Once you choose one of these options you can't then place text in that area. It's one or the other. (Although you could add a text box to the slide and put in text that way if you wanted. That's intermediate-level so we're not going to cover it here but the option can be found in the Text section of the Insert tab.)

We're not going to cover all of those options in this guide, just adding a table and inserting a picture, but they all work on the same principle and it's good to know they exist.

Alright, then. On to adding a table.

Tables

The first option in that set of images is Insert Table.

Click on it and you'll see the Insert Table dialogue box. It lets you specify the number of columns and rows you want in your table. Below you can see the dialogue box as well as the table that was inserted into the slide using five columns and five rows after I clicked on OK.

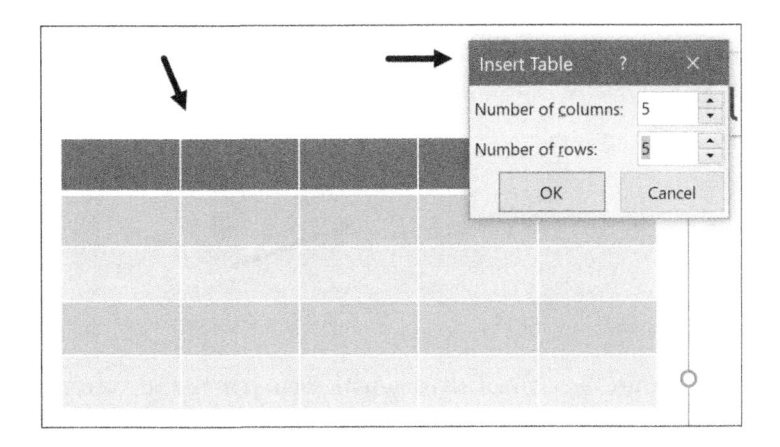

Background Color

By default for this theme, the first row is in a different color because it's a header row for the table. The remaining rows are in alternating colors.

The colors used are consistent with the presentation theme. You can change the colors used in your table under the Table Tools Design tab.

75

The Table Styles options provide various layouts that use the color palette of the presentation theme. Or you can select all of the cells in the table or a subset of cells, like a row, and use the Shading option to choose a new background color that way.

The Shape Fill option in the mini formatting menu can also be used to change the background color of selected cells.

Font Color

Font color should be set to work with the original background colors. For example on this table the header row uses a white font color but the main body of the table uses a black font color.

That color can be changed on the Home tab or via the mini formatting menu just like any other text. Either select the text you want to change first or make the color change after you click into a cell but before you start typing.

Add Text or Numbers to Your Table

To add information to the table, click into any of the cells in the table and start typing. If you enter text that is wider than the width of the column, it will automatically flow down to another line and the row height will change to make sure all of the text is visible. Like so:

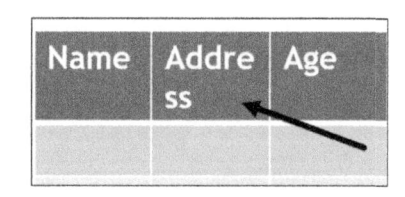

Name	Address	Age

You may need to change your column widths or font size when this happens to better display the text since, as you can see above, having the word "Address" break across that line is not ideal.

If you have your information in an existing table in Word or Excel, you can copy the information from that table into PowerPoint by highlighting the cells in Word or Excel, using copy (Ctrl + C), and then clicking into the first cell in the PowerPoint table where you want to place that information and using paste (Ctrl + V).

If the data you want to paste into your presentation has more columns than the table, PowerPoint will add additional columns. Same with the number of

Tables

rows. The text in the table will resize to fit on the slide, so it's best to bring in your information first and then format from there.

If you have fewer columns or rows, PowerPoint will just paste your data into the number of columns or rows needed for the data.

PowerPoint is not set up to format numbers well, so I find that it is easier when dealing with numeric data to do that in Excel.

Align Text Within Cells

If after you've entered text into your table you want to change the alignment of the text so that it's centered or left-aligned, etc. you can do this by highlighting the cells you want to change, going to the Table Tools Layout tab, and going to the Alignment section.

The top row where you see the three options with lines is where you can choose to left-align, center, or right-align text. The second row where you see the three boxes with lines in them is where you can choose to place text at the top, center, or bottom of each cell.

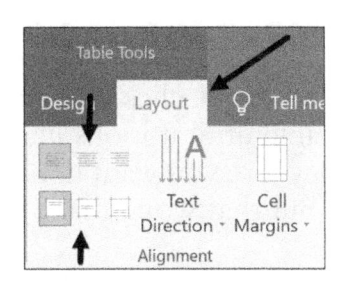

Add Rows or Columns

If you need additional rows in your table, simply use the tab key from the last cell in the last row of the table and PowerPoint will add a new line.

You can also highlight a row, go to the Rows & Columns section of the Table Tools Layout tab, and choose Insert Above or Insert Below.

To add a column, highlight an existing column and choose Insert Left or Insert Right.

You can also highlight a row or column and right-click to bring up the mini formatting menu which has an Insert dropdown with all four choices.

Delete Rows or Columns

To delete a row or column from a table, you can highlight the row or column and use the backspace key. You can also highlight the row or column and then right-click and choose Cut or use the Delete dropdown menu on the mini formatting menu.

Another option is to click into a cell in that row or column, go to the Table Tools Layout tab, and under the Rows & Columns section click on the dropdown arrow under Delete. From there you can choose Delete Columns, Delete Rows, or Delete Table.

Delete the Table

To delete the entire table, right-click on the table and use the Delete option in the mini formatting menu to choose Delete Table.

Or right-click on the table and choose Select Table from the dropdown and then use the Delete or Backspace key.

Or click on the table and then use the Delete dropdown in the Rows & Columns section of the Table Tools Layout tab.

Move the Table

Click on the table to select it. Or right-click and choose Select Table. Hold your mouse over the edge of the table until it looks like a four-sided arrow and then left-click and drag the table to where you want it. Keep in mind that you can drag it on top of another text box but that won't make it part of that text box.

Column Width

To change the width of a column, click on a cell in the column and go to the Cell Size section of the Table Tools Layout tab and change the value for Width. This will change the overall width of the table.

You can also hold your mouse over the right-hand side of the column in the table itself until the cursor looks like two parallel lines with arrows pointing off to the sides and then left-click and drag to your desired width. This will change the width of that column and the one to its right, but not the overall size of the table unless you were resizing the final column in the table.

You can also double-left click along that edge to get the column to automatically resize to the width of the text that's currently in the column. This will also change the width of the table at the same time.

Row Height

To change the height of a row, click on a cell in the row and go to the Cell Size section of Table Tools Layout tab and change the value for Height. You cannot change a row height to a value that would hide any text in that row.

Another option is to hold your mouse over the bottom edge of the row in the table itself until the cursor looks like two parallel lines with arrows pointing up and down and then left-click and drag to your desired height. Once again, you will be limited in how short you can make the row by any existing text in that row and also by the font size for text in that row.

With both methods, only the height of that row will change which means the table height will also change.

Resize the Table

To change the dimensions of an entire table, you can click on the table and then left-click and drag from any of the white circles around the edge of the table. Be sure that you have a white double-sided arrow when you do so or you may just end up moving the table around.

Clicking on one of the white circles in the corner will allow you to resize the table proportionately as long as you click and drag at an angle.

You can also click on the table and go to the Table Tools Layout tab and change the dimensions for the table in the Table Size section.

If you want to resize the table and have the relative height and width of the table stay the same, click the Lock Aspect Ratio box first. When you do that PowerPoint will adjust both measurements at once to keep the ratio of height to width for the table constant.

Split Cells in a Table

You can take one or more cells in a table and split them into multiple cells. To do this, highlight the cell or cells you want to split, go to the Table Tools Layout tab, and click on Split Cells in the Merge section.

This will bring up the Split Cells dialogue box which lets you specify how many columns and rows you want each cell split into.

The choice you make will apply to each cell you selected. So if you select four cells and tell it to split them into two columns and one row, each of those four cells will be split into two columns and one row giving you eight cells total.

You can also bring up the Split Cells dialogue box by right-clicking and choosing Split Cells from the dropdown menu.

Merge Cells in a Table

You can also merge cells in a table which combines the selected cells into one.

In this case, highlight the cells that you want to merge, go to the Table Tools Layout tab, and choose Merge Cells from the Merge section. All of the cells will be combined into one and any text that was in those cells will be shown in the newly-merged cell with one row per line of text working from left to right and top to bottom of the old cell range.

Another option is to select the cells you want to merge, right-click, and choose Merge Cells from the dropdown menu.

Table Design

We already touched on this a bit, but the Table Tools Design tab will let you control the appearance of your table.

You can change the borders around and within your table using the Borders dropdown. Before you apply a border be sure to change the line width, style, and color in the Draw Borders section if you want those settings to be different from the default settings..

Also, the Table Style Options section will let you turn on or off banded rows in your table. (This is where each row of the table has an alternating color.)

You can also turn on or off banded columns which applies alternating colors to each column.

I do not recommend having alternating rows and alternating columns on at the same time.

In the Table Style Options section you can also adjust the settings so that the last row (total row), first column, or last column are formatted differently by checking the boxes for those options.

Pictures

The option directly below Insert Table is Pictures. Click on it and you'll see the Insert Picture dialogue box. By default it will open in your Pictures folder on your computer, but you can navigate from there to any location where the picture you want is stored.

If you click on the All Pictures dropdown option next to the File Name box you can see the picture file types that PowerPoint will accept. (Which looks to be pretty much any type you can image.)

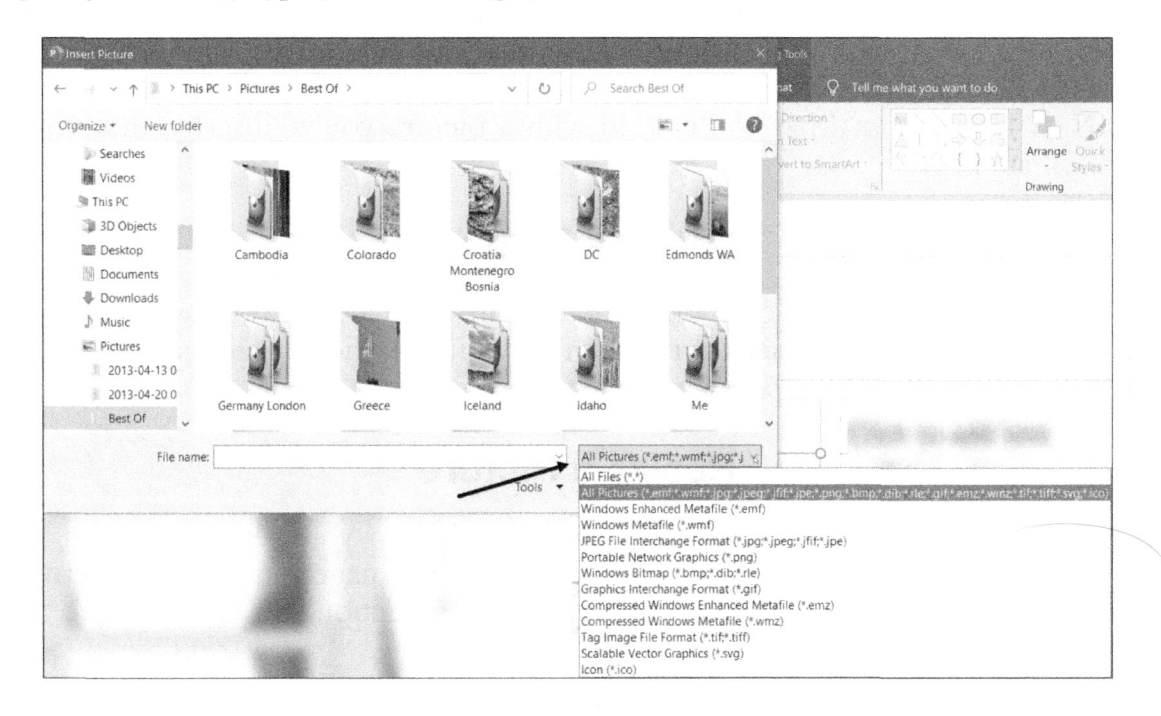

81

Navigate to where the picture you want is saved, click on the picture, and then choose Insert. This will insert that picture into that text box. It will be centered.

You can also click on the arrow next to Insert and choose to link your photo instead, but I'd generally advise against that because it's far too easy to break a link like that. For example, you link to an image and then copy your presentation to a thumb drive so you can use it on the provided laptop at the conference center and suddenly there are no images in your presentation and you're standing in front of five hundred people not knowing why. (Or knowing why but also knowing it's too late to fix it.)

Better usually to just put the image into your presentation. The reasons to link instead of insert are if you think the image may be updated at some point outside of PowerPoint or if you are using a large number of images and need to keep the file size down. For a printed presentation it won't be a problem. For a presentation you're presenting be sure you have access to those images at the time of your presentation.

Okay, then.

The image you chose will insert into your slide at a size that fits within the text box where you chose to insert it. If the image is smaller than the active area it will insert at its current size, but if it's larger than the active area it will be scaled down.

(This is for when you use the Pictures icon to insert an image into a text box. You can also go to the Insert tab and choose Pictures from the Images section there to insert a picture on a blank slide. In that case the image you insert will be centered in the presentation slide and may fit the entire slide if it's large enough.)

Now let's discuss what you can do with a picture you've inserted into your presentation.

Move a Picture

To move your image, left-click on it and drag it to the location you want. (It will take the text box it was inserted into with it, but if you then delete the image, the text box will reappear in its original location.)

Resize a Picture

You can also resize a picture after you insert it into your slide. If you have specific dimensions that you want to use, click on the image and go to the Picture Tools Format tab. At the far end you'll see the Size section.

Pictures

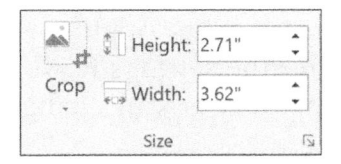

Change either the height or the width and the image will resize proportionately, meaning that PowerPoint will adjust the other measurement to keep the height to width ratio the same. This is a good thing because it prevents the image from becoming distorted or skewed.

You can also click onto the image and then left-click on any of the white circles around the perimeter and drag until the image is the size you want. This will not resize the image proportionately, so you can easily end up with a distorted image if you do it this way. But if you click on a corner and drag at an angle that usually will keep the height and width proportional because you are resizing the image on both dimensions at once. (If you don't like the result, use Ctrl + Z to undo.)

Another option is to right-click on the image and choose Size and Position. This will open a Format Picture task pane on the right-hand side of your workspace, which includes fields for Height and Width. You can uncheck the Lock Aspect Ratio box if you want to change one measure independent of the other.

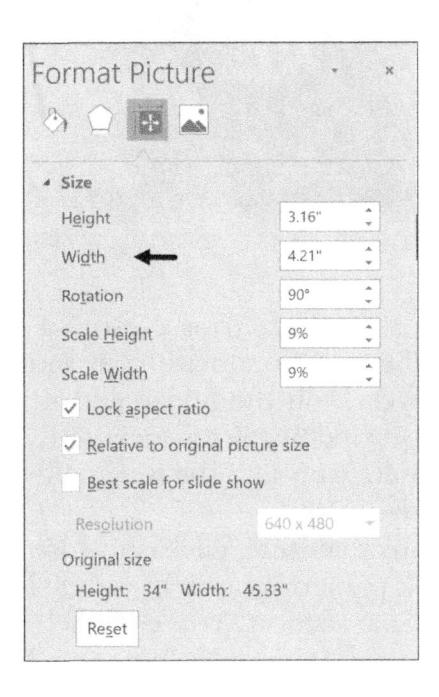

83

Also, you can reset the image to its original appearance from here, but be careful because that will remove the settings PowerPoint applied to the image as well. So if it resized it to fit that text box or changed the image orientation, that will be lost too.

The Format Picture task pane can also be accessed by clicking on the expansion arrow in the Size section of the Picture Tools Format tab.

Rotate a Picture

If you want to rotate the picture that you inserted, click on the image and then click on the little white outline of an arrow circling to the right that will be visible along the edge or top of the image.

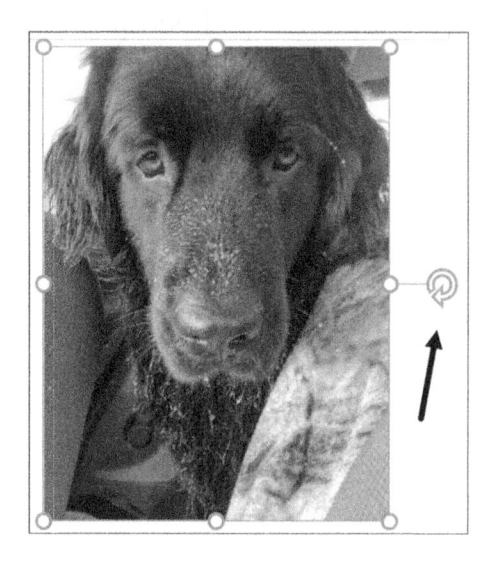

Click and hold this while you move your cursor in the direction you want to rotate the image and it will rotate along with your mouse.

Your other option is to click on the image and then go to the Picture Tools Format tab and click on the dropdown arrow next to Rotate in the Arrange section.

You can choose from there to rotate the image 90 degrees right or left or flip the image vertically or horizontally.

If you need more options than that, click on More Rotation Options to bring up the Format Picture task pane on the right-hand side of the screen. Rotation is the third option in the Size section. You can click into the box there and set the rotation to any value you want from 1 degree to 360 degrees.

Pictures

(Technically it lets you set a value from -3600 degrees to 3600 degrees, but a circle is only 360 degrees, so…)

Crop a Picture

Sometimes I'll drop a picture into a presentation and then realize that I didn't want the entire picture, I just wanted a section of it. (This is especially true when I take screenshots of Excel using Print Screen and then want to just keep a small section of that screenshot for my presentation.) In those cases, I need to crop the image to only show the portion I care about.

To crop an image, right-click on the image and choose Crop from the mini formatting bar. You should then see small black bars on each side of the image and at the corners. Be sure when you click and drag that the cursor looks like a bar, because otherwise you might end up resizing the image instead. (If so, Ctrl + Z to undo and try again.)

Left-click on those bars and drag until only the portion of the image that you want to keep is fully visible. (The area that will be cropped away will be grayed out but still partially visible like bottom portion of the image below.)

To permanently apply the crop to your image, click away or hit Esc.

If you start to crop your image and realize that you want a different portion of the image in the visible area, you can click and drag on the image to move it around. The part that will remain after you finish will still be fully visible but the rest will be grayed out.

This is especially useful if you insert an image and PowerPoint crops the image for you, because it doesn't always know what part of the image you want visible. Choosing to crop but not actually doing so will let you move that image around until the portion of the image you want visible is in the active area.

Your other option for cropping is to go to the Picture Tools Format tab and choose Crop from the Size section. The first option in the dropdown is a simple crop.

For an image that's already been cropped, the full image will appear with the cropped space already marked. This makes it relatively easy to fix the cropping of an image if you get it wrong the first time since you can just choose to crop again and then drag the image or the bars to the correct location.

In the Crop dropdown in the Picture Tools Format tab you also have the option to crop to a shape or crop to a specific aspect ratio but those are more advanced options that we're not going to cover here.

Bring Forward/Send Backward

If you are ever in a situation where you have images or text boxes that overlap (which if you're using a standard template would only happen if you moved something around), you may need to use the bring forward or send backward options.

Visualize the layers of text and images in your presentation as a stack of playing cards. You're only going to see what's visible from the top of the stack. Which means if you shuffle those cards into a different order, you will see something different.

So, for example, if you have a layer with a picture that you want to be in the background of a layer with text, then you would want to place the picture layer behind the text layer. You could do this by using one of the Send Backward options to position the layer with the picture behind the layer with text.

You could get the same result by using one of the Bring Forward options on the text layer.

The Bring Forward and Send Backward options are available in the Arrange section of the Picture Tools Format tab. There is a dropdown for each one.

Send Backward has the choice to Send Backward, which will move a layer back one spot, or to Send to Back, which will make that layer the bottom layer.

Bring Forward has the option to Bring Forward, which will move a layer up one spot, or Bring to Front, which will make it the topmost layer.

The Bring Forward and Send Backward options are also available by right-clicking on an image and choosing them from the dropdown menu.

Pictures

I should note here that sometimes Bring Forward and Send Backward didn't perform the way I expected them to, but Bring to Front and Send to Back always did. So if you get stuck with that issue as well, you should be able to stack your layers in any order you want by strategically applying the Bring to Front and Send to Back options. Not as easy, but it works.

Alignment

You can align images to one another or you can align them with respect to the presentation slide itself. If you're using a template and bringing in images as part of a text box, you shouldn't really need to use this, but the option does exist under the Align option in the Arrange section of the Picture Tools Format tab.

You can choose to align left (place the image along the left-hand side of the slide), align center (place the image in the center of the slide as judged from left to right), align right (place the image along the right-hand side of the slide), align top (place the image along the top edge of the slide), align middle (place the image in the center of the slide as judged from top to bottom), or align bottom (place the image along the bottom edge of the slide).

Distribute horizontally will center the image judged from left to right. Distribute vertically will center the image judged from top to bottom. Where this one matters is when you have multiple images selected at once. If you have multiple images selected at once then it will take those images and distribute them either across the width of the slide (horizontally) or from top to bottom (vertically) so that there is equal space between the images and the edges of the slide.

If you do have multiple images, you can select those images, and then under Align choose Align Selected Objects and instead of aligning the objects to the presentation slide it will align them to one another. So, for example, align right would move the left-hand object into alignment with the right-hand object.

Picture Styles

There is a Picture Styles section in the Picture Tools Format tab. Most of the styles involve placing a frame around the image, but some of them also involve skewing the image or adding a shadow to the image so that it looks three-dimensional.

To apply a picture style, click on your image and go the Picture Styles section of the Picture Tools Format tab. Hold your mouse over each style to see what it will look like when applied to your image. Click on one if you want to actually apply it.

Adjust a Picture

PowerPoint provides a number of options for adjusting an image. As with most things, I will advise you against getting too out of control with the special effects. There are industries where that may be warranted, but most times you want to present your information in as clear and succinct a way as possible.

Having said that, click on an image and then go to the Picture Tools Format tab and you'll see on the far left-hand side that there is a section called Adjust.

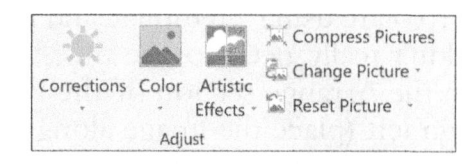

The Corrections option will allow you to sharpen or soften an image as well as adjust the brightness/contrast of the image.

The Color option will allow you to change the saturation or tone of your image as well as recolor your image.

Artistic Effects allows you to adjust your image so that it looks like a marker drawing, pencil sketch, etc.

For all three options, click on the dropdown arrow to see how each choice will impact your image.

(As a side note, if you really need to do something like this I'd recommend using an image software program instead and then bringing in the already-edited image but I do know that some people do design work in PowerPoint itself. This is where you'd go to do so.)

Animations

If you have a presentation slide with multiple bullet points it's often very useful to have those bullet points appear one at a time. This way people listen to what you're saying instead of trying to read ahead on the slide and see what you're going to say next.

To do this, first go to the slide where you want to add animation. Next, click on the first line of text that you want to have appear and go to the Animations tab. Click on one of the options in the Animation section.

I recommend using Appear. It simply shows the line without any fancy tricks which can be distracting.

Once you apply animation to one bulleted point in your slide, PowerPoint will apply it to the remainder of the items in your slide.

The order in which those items will appear is shown by the way they are numbered. All items numbered 1 will appear first, then all items numbered 2, then all items numbered 3, etc.

So in the example below we have three bulleted items, each of which will appear one at a time starting with the top bullet.

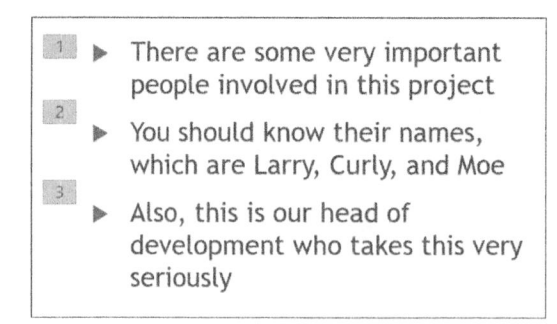

> 1 ▶ There are some very important people involved in this project
>
> 2 ▶ You should know their names, which are Larry, Curly, and Moe
>
> 3 ▶ Also, this is our head of development who takes this very seriously

The appearance of the next item is usually triggered by hitting Enter, using the down arrow on your keyboard, or left-clicking to advance through the slide as you present.

If you have indented lines of text, so sub-bullets, you will probably need to fix their numbering because by default they will appear at the same time as their "parent" line.

This is probably best understood visually. See below:

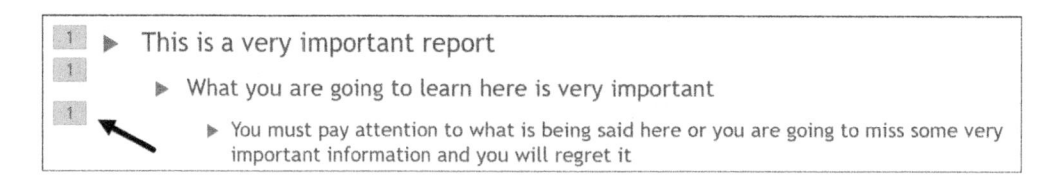

> 1 ▶ This is a very important report
> 1 ▶ What you are going to learn here is very important
> 1 ▶ You must pay attention to what is being said here or you are going to miss some very important information and you will regret it

All three lines of text in the image above have a 1 next to them. That means they're all going to appear together which I generally do not want because that means my audience will be reading ahead instead of listening to me.

To fix this, click into the slide, go to the Animations tab and click on the expansion arrow for the Animation section.

This will bring up the Appear dialogue box.

In that dialogue box, click on the Text Animation tab, which is the third one. There will be a dropdown option at the top labeled Group Text. Click on that and choose one of the other grouping levels.

Animations

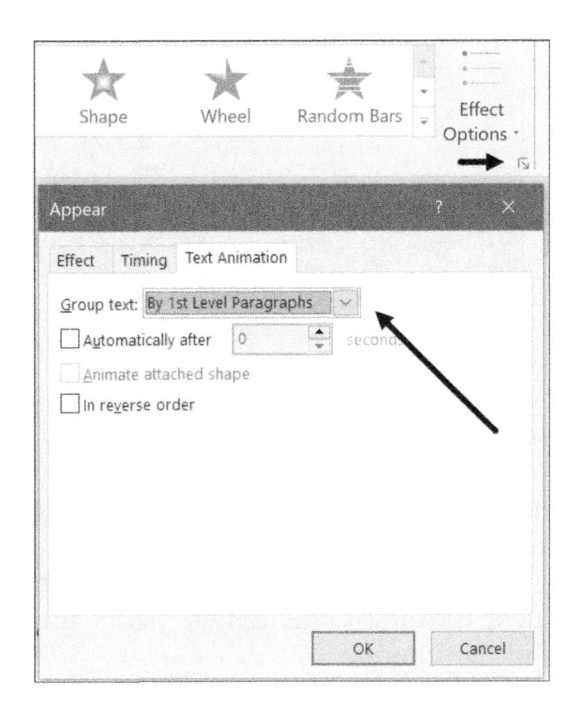

Depending on how many levels of bullets you have on the slide you will probably need the "By 2nd Level Paragraphs" or the "By 3rd Level Paragraphs" option to get all lines of text to appear individually. Once you've made your choice, click on OK.

The slide will now show adjusted numbering based upon your choice. With 3rd Level Paragraphs that means the first three level of bullets are treated as separate lines that appear one at a time instead of grouped together.

By default, a picture will appear when the slide appears. If instead you want your picture to appear after your text, then you need to also apply animation to the picture. You do so the same way you would with your text by clicking on an animation choice in the Animation tab.

If the picture is the first item you applied animation to it will be numbered 1. If you apply animation to it after you apply animation to your text, it will be set to appear after all of your text.

To change the order in which your different elements appear on the slide, go to the Animations tab and click on Animation Pane in the Advanced Animation section.

This will bring up the Animation Pane task pane, which will show all of your elements and the order in which they appear.

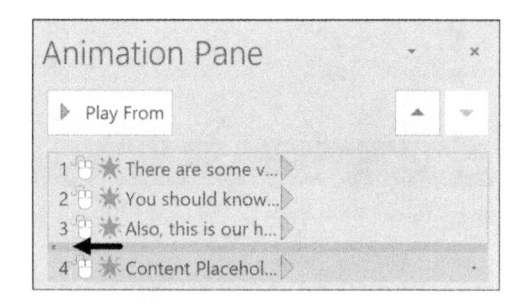

(You may have to click on the small double arrow under a numbered section to see all of your numbered options from your slide. In the image above I've already done that so clicking on it again would hide them.)

To change the order of your elements, click on one of the elements listed and then use the up and down arrows at the top to move that element up or down.

You can also change the level at which your text is grouped in this pane by clicking on the arrow next to one of the text elements and then choosing Effect Options from the dropdown menu.

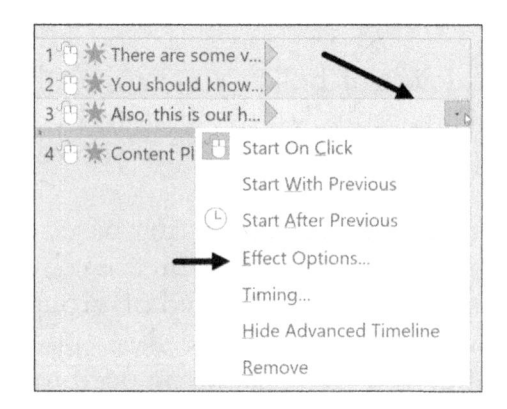

That will bring up the Appear dialogue box.

If you want to have some of your bullet points appear together but others appear separately, the best way I know to do this is to set up the slide as if everything will appear separately and then highlight the rows you want to have appear together and click on your chosen animation option once more. This will change the numbering of those items so that they all are grouped together.

There are other things you can do with animation that we're not going to cover here, such as have each bullet point appear on its own on a timed schedule. But for this beginner guide I just wanted you to know how to structure your slides so that each point you want to make appears separately.

Animations

If you click on the downward-pointing arrow with a line under it to expand the animations box you'll see that there is actually a variety of animation choices. Some animations are for bringing in text or images, some are for emphasizing what's already there, and some are for taking it away. The different categories are color-coded with green for entrance, yellow for emphasis, and red for exit.

You can see what each animation will look like by applying it. It will automatically run once when you do so. If it doesn't or you want to see it again later, click on the Preview option in the left-hand corner of the Animations tab and your animations for that slide should re-run.

I know it's tempting to try to make a presentation more interesting with things like this, but if you can't engage your audience with what you're saying then fix what you're saying instead.

I would strongly urge you to keep to just using Appear as your animation option. You can absolutely have your bullet points fly in or even bounce in (please, no), but ask yourself if that's appropriate for your audience.

If you're presenting to first graders, sure, have a bullet point bounce in. But a potential business client? Eh. Or a group of your professional peers? Uh-uh. Don't do it. Don't fall for the temptation.

Okay since we're talking about how to make a presentation "professional", let's talk about a few design principles to keep in mind as well while we're at it.

Design Principles

I've touched on this a few times, but I think it's good to take a chapter and discuss some basic design principles to keep in mind as you're preparing your presentation. I'm going to assume here that you're actually intending to use your PowerPoint presentation as a presentation. Meaning, you're going to talk through it and not expect it to talk for you, and that the slides are going to be presented on a projector of some sort to a live audience.

(In other words, I'm not addressing the consulting model of using PowerPoint where you put together a weekly client presentation on a series of slides that you hand out to your client and pack full of information and then walk through even though the client could just read the darned things themselves without paying you thousands of dollars for you to be there while they do it.)

Font Size

Make sure that all of the text on your slide will be visible to anyone in the room. I'd try to have all of the text be 14 point or larger if you can manage it.

Font Type

As with all other design elements it can be tempting to use a fancy font. Resist the temptation. You want a basic, clear, easy-to-read font for your presentation elements. This means using something like Arial or Calibri or Times New Roman instead of something like Algerian.

Summaries Instead of Explanations

The text on your slide should be there as a general outline of what you're going to say, not contain the full text of what you want to say. Think of each bullet point as a prompt that you can look at to trigger your recollection.

The reason you do it this way is because people will try to read whatever you put in front of them. So if you give them a slide full of text they will be busy reading that text rather than listening to what you have to say.

Also, if it's all on the slide, why listen to you at all?

So use the text on your slide as a high-level summary of your next point instead of as an explanation.

For example, I might have a slide titled "The Three Stages of Money Laundering" and then list on that slide three bullet points, "Placement", "Layering", and "Integration". As I show each bullet point I'll discuss what each of those stages is and how it works. If I feel a need to really go into detail then I'll have a separate slide for each one where I provide further information in small bite-sized chunks.

Contrast

You want your text to be visible. Which means you have to think about contrast. If you have a dark background, then use a light-colored text. For example, dark blue background, white text. If you have a light background, use a dark-colored text. For example, white background, black text.

And beware of anything that could trip up someone with color-blindness. So no red on green or green on red and no blue on yellow or yellow on blue.

Also, and this may be more of a personal preference, but I try to use the slide templates that have white for the background behind the text portions of my slides. I'm fine with colorful borders and colorful header sections, but where the meat of the presentation is I prefer to have a white background often with black text. (That's the easiest combination to read.)

So I'll choose the Ion Boardroom theme before I'll choose the Ion theme, for example.

Don't Get Cute

PowerPoint has a lot of bells and whistles. You can have lines of text that fly in and slide in and fade away. Or slides that flash in or appear through bars. And some of the templates it provides are downright garish.

Design Principles

Resist the urge to overdo it.

Ask yourself every time you're tempted to add some special effect if adding it will improve the effectiveness of your presentation. And ask yourself what your boss's boss's boss would think of your presentation. I've worked in banking and regulatory environments and I will tell you there is little appreciation in those environments for overly-bright colors and flashy special effects. (Whereas some tech company environment where the CEO wears jeans and t-shirts to work may be all for that kind of thing. Know your audience.)

I do think that using the animation option to have one bullet point appear at a time is a good idea. But you can do that with the Appear option. You don't need Fade, Fly In, Float In, Split, Wipe, etc.

And, yes, it can sometimes feel boring to use the same animation for a hundred slides in a row. But remember the point of your presentation is to convey information to your audience. Anything that doesn't help you do that should go.

Other Tips and Tricks

Now that we've walked through the basics of creating your presentation, let's cover a few other things you might want to do, starting with adding notes to your slides.

Add Notes To A Slide

If you add notes to your slides you can then print a notes version of those slides that lets you see not just the slide that your audience sees but any additional comments. So if you're worried about forgetting something but don't want too much text on your slide? Put it in a note.

There is also a display option that lets you see the notes on your screen but not have them appear to the audience. Either one is a great option when you have points you want to be sure to make but don't want to clutter up your slides.

To use notes, though, you first have to add them.

The Notes portion of the presentation is not visible by default, but if you look at the bottom middle of your workspace you should see a little item that says Notes. Click on that and a task pane that says "Click to add notes" will open below your slide.

Click there and start typing to add your notes.

The other option to open or close the Notes task pane is to go to the Show section of the View tab and click on Notes. If the task pane was already open it will close, if it wasn't it will appear.

Spellcheck

It's always a good idea to run spellcheck on anything you create for an audience. To check the spelling in your document, go to the Proofing section of the Review tab and click on Spelling. (It's on the far left-hand side.)

PowerPoint will then walk through your entire document flagging spelling errors and repeated words.

If there are no errors you'll see a dialogue box that tells you the spell check is complete. Click OK to close it.

If there are errors, the Spelling task pane will open and for each one PowerPoint will show a suggested change and highlight the word it flagged in the slide itself. For example, here I had the word "is" twice in a row:

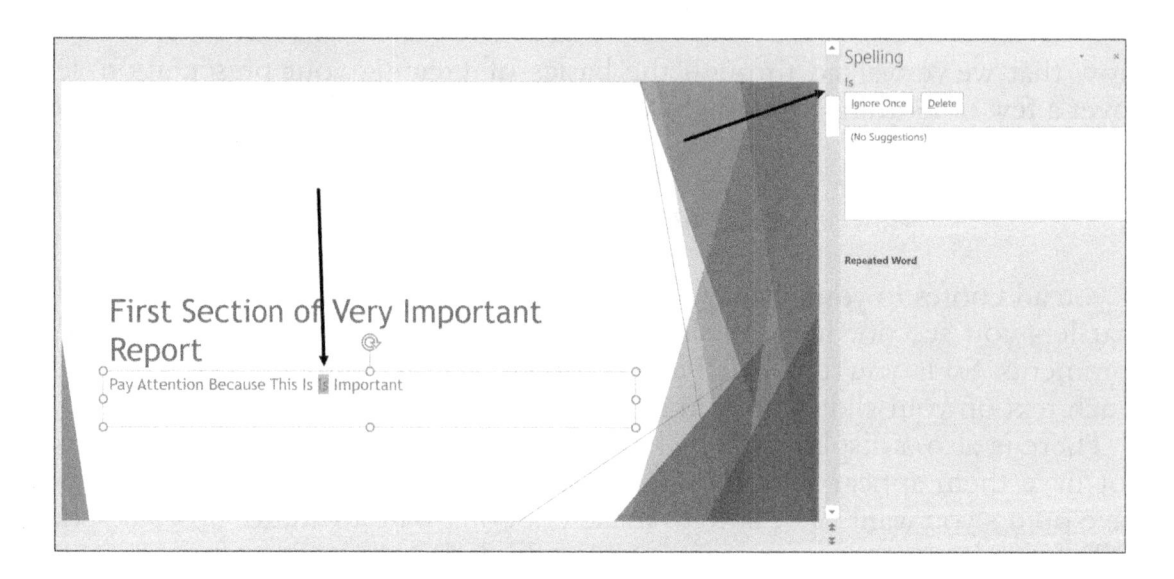

If you don't want to make the suggested change, click on Ignore.

For spelling errors PowerPoint will give you the choice to Ignore All or to Ignore Once. Ignore Once when you just want it to skip this one instance; Ignore All when you want it to skip the word everywhere it occurs in the presentation. For example, I often have to tell Office programs to ignore my first name because it almost always flags it as a spelling error.

That does bring up the third option you'll get with a spelling error which is Add. This will add the word to your version of PowerPoint's dictionary so that the word is never flagged as a spelling error again. So if there's some term that's common to your industry but not in the PowerPoint dictionary you can add the

Other Tips and Tricks

word and then it won't be flagged in any of your presentations. In contrast, Ignore All just applies to the current presentation.

For any issues it flags, PowerPoint will suggest solutions, like above where it gave the option to delete the duplicate word. Click on that option to apply the solution.

With spelling errors, if it can identify a close enough word it will suggest alternatives like here where I misspelled "regret" as "regert" and it suggested four possible words I might have meant.

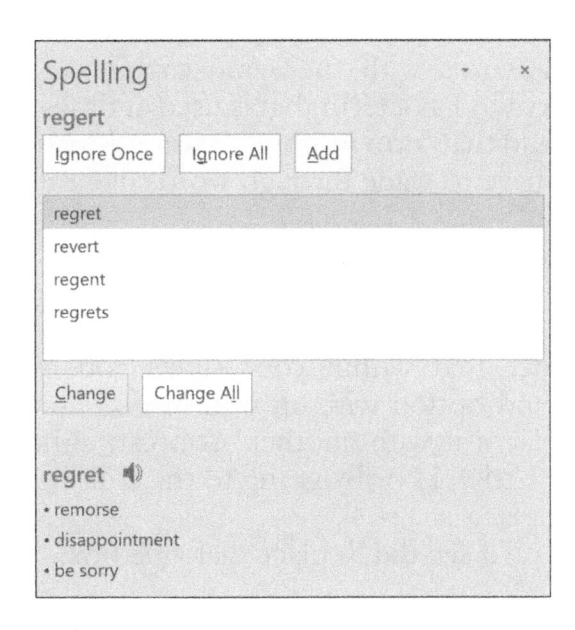

```
Spelling
regert
[Ignore Once]  [Ignore All]  [Add]

regret
revert
regent
regrets

[Change]  [Change All]

regret 🔊
• remorse
• disappointment
• be sorry
```

To replace the current word with one of the suggestions, click on the suggested word and then click on Change to change this one instance or Change All to change all uses of the misspelled word in the document.

Be careful with Change All and Ignore All. It's possible to miss an error by using one of those options. Also, spellcheck is not infallible. There are times when I've spelled a word wrong but it created another word that was in the dictionary and so PowerPoint didn't flag it. (I really do wish they had spellcheck for certain lowkey cusswords since at least one seems to be pretty easy to use inadvertently.) A good reminder to always read your presentation when you're done. Technology can only do so much.

101

Find

If you need to find a specific reference in your slides you can use Find to do so. The Find option is in the Editing section of the Home tab (on the far right-hand side). Click on Find and the Find dialogue box will appear.

You can also open the Find dialogue box by using Ctrl + F.

Type the word you want into the white text box under "Find What" and then click on Find Next. PowerPoint will walk you through the entire document moving to the next instance of that word each time you click on Find Next.

You can sometimes save time by choosing to just search for whole words only or to just search for words with the same capitalization (match case). For example, in my industry CAT is a term that is used at times for consolidated audit trail. When I want to find that term in a presentation I match case and find whole words only so I don't have to wade through words like catastrophe or catalog.

Replace Text

If you need to replace text within your slides you can use Replace. This essentially pairs the Find option with an option that takes the word you were searching for and replaces it with another. You can either launch the Replace dialogue box by using Ctrl + H or by going to the Editing section of the Home tab and clicking on Replace.

When you do this you'll see the Replace dialogue box.

The "Find what" box is what you are looking for. The "Replace with" box is what you want to put in its place.

The match case and find whole words only options are helpful when using Find but essential when using Replace. I have seen more than one very awkward instance of replace that went wrong. For example, I mentioned above that CAT

Other Tips and Tricks

is a term I might search for. Think what would happen if I replaced all instances of "cat" with "consolidated audit trail" including in the word catalog.

For replace you can replace your instances of a word one at a time by using the Replace option or you can replace them all at once using Replace All. Be careful with this. And be sure to read the whole presentation if you use Replace All.

Replacing text is easy to do and easy to mess up.

Replace Font

If you go to the Editing section of the Home tab and click on the dropdown arrow next to Replace you'll see that there is an option there to Replace Fonts.

Click on that option to bring up the Replace Font dialogue box. It will show you two dropdown menus.

The first dropdown is where you select the font that is in your presentation that you want to replace. It should only show the fonts used in your presentation. (But don't worry if it shows one or two you didn't think you were using. They may be used somewhere you can't see.)

The second dropdown is where you choose the font you want to replace it with.

Once you've selected both fonts, click on Replace and every usage of the first font will be replaced with the second font. This can come in very handy if you have a corporate requirement to use a specific font that wasn't followed when the presentation was created. (Ask me how I know…)

Just be sure to then look back through your presentation and make sure everything looks "right", because different fonts take up different amounts of space. It's possible that changing over the font could impact the appearance of your slides.

Presentation Size

PowerPoint gives you the choice between two presentation sizes. The standard size is 4:3 and the widescreen size is 16:9. You can also choose a custom slide size.

All of these choices are available in the Customize section of the Design tab on the far right side where it says Slide Size. Click on the dropdown arrow to make your choice.

(If you click on the Custom Slide Size option you can even make a presentation that is in portrait orientation, so like a normal printed report, rather than in landscape orientation. Although, if you're going to do this do it before you start putting together your slides or you'll have a complete mess to fix up. This would not be a good choice for a presentation that's going to be projected on a screen, but could be an interesting idea for a printed presentation.)

Present Your Slides

When it comes time to do your presentation, chances are someone will hook up a laptop with your presentation on it to a projector. By default that will show your computer screen. But you don't want someone to see what you've been seeing this whole time as you built your presentation. You just want them to see the slides and nothing else.

Which means you need to go into presentation mode.

To do this, go to the Slide Show tab. On the left-hand side you have the Start Slide Show section. If you click on From Beginning, this will start a presentation at the first slide in your PowerPoint presentation. If you click on From Current Slide it will start the presentation at the slide that's currently visible.

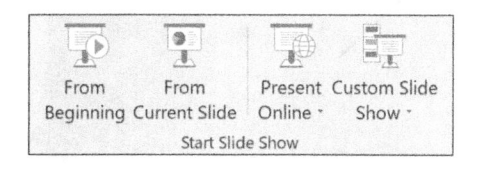

F5 will also start your presentation from the beginning. And Shift + F5 will start your presentation from your current slide.

Either choice will launch the slides you've created as a full-screen presentation.

There are a number of ways to navigate through your presentation. You can use Enter, left-click, page down, or the down arrow to move to the next slide or bullet point. You can use page up or the up arrow to move to the previous slide or bullet point.

You can also right-click and choose Next or Previous from the dropdown menu.

The PowerPoint screen you've been working in will still be there and open behind the scenes. You can reach it using Alt + Tab to move through your active windows or you can use Esc to close the presentation.

Before you enter presentation mode, I'd recommend having any additional windows you're going to want open already so you can easily access them using Alt + Tab.

And it's always a good idea to run through your presentation slides before you present to anyone so you can check and make sure that all the animations, etc. are working.

There is an option to view your slides in Presenter View. What this does is show on your computer screen the slide the audience can currently see as well as your slide notes and the next slide, but on the presentation screen only the presentation slide will show.

Because I'm currently using both an external monitor and my laptop, when I launch a presentation this happens automatically.

If you don't want that, you can go to the presenter screen and in Display settings change it to Duplicate Slide View. This will make it so both screens just show the presentation

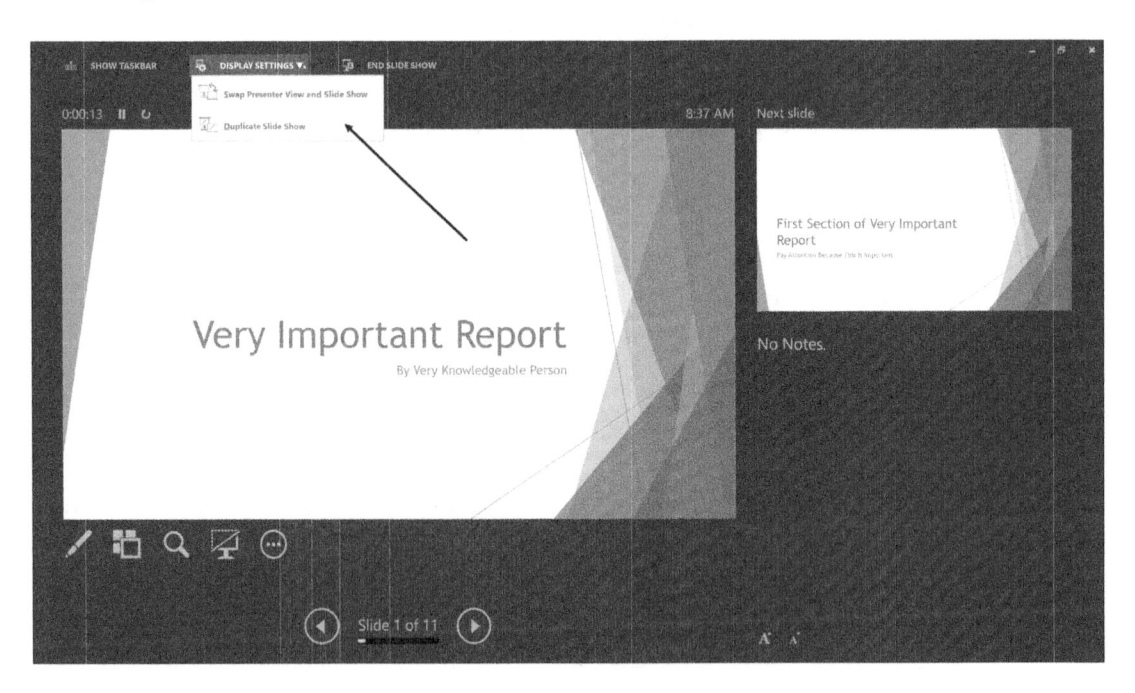

Present Your Slides

If you need to switch which screen shows which information, choose Swap Presenter View and Slide Show. (Just be aware that if you do this in front of a live audience and you're using notes that they will see any notes you have.)

You can also show and hide presenter view by right-clicking on your presentation and choosing that option from the dropdown.

To close a presentation, hit Esc. Or, right-click and choose End Show from the dropdown menu.

That's the basics of presenting. There are more advanced options, like setting up your slides to advance on a schedule, that are more advanced topics.

Print Your Presentation

You have the option to print your presentation slides, your presentation slides as handouts (so with room for people to take notes), or your presentation slides with your notes.

To do any of these, type Ctrl + P or go to the File tab and then choose Print on the left-hand side.

Both choices will bring you to the Print screen.

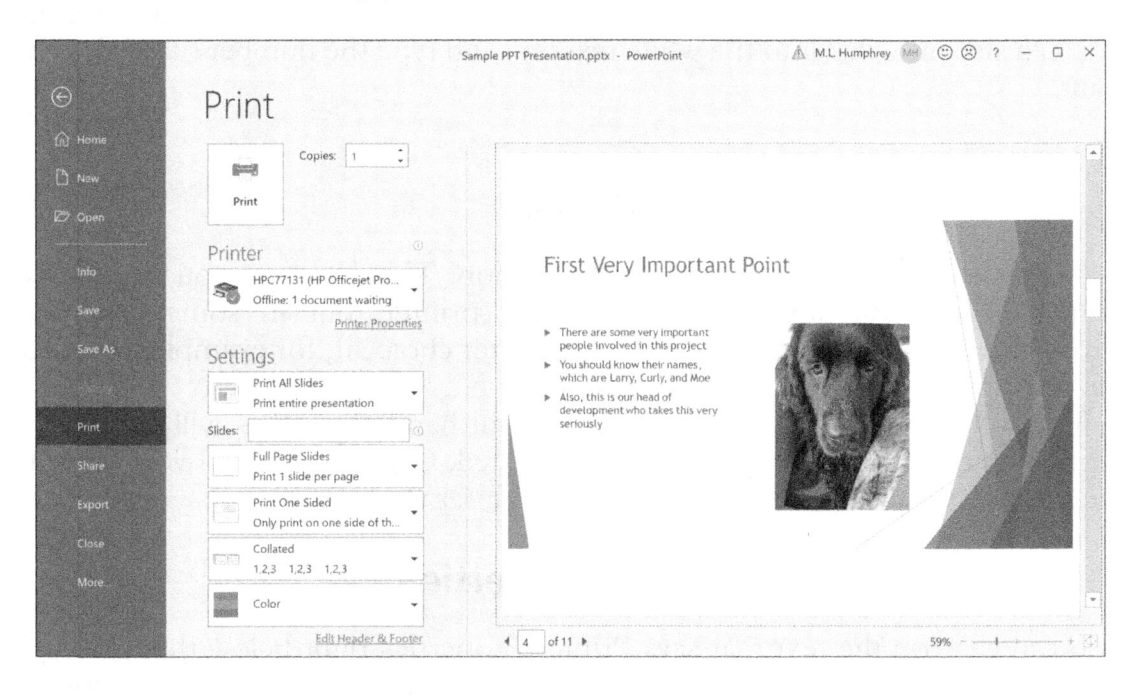

On the left-hand side are your File tab choices, next you'll see a printer icon with a number of setting choices below that, and then on the right-hand side will be a preview of the current slide. You can use the numbers and arrows below that to navigate between your slides.

The default is to print all of your slides and in full-page format and that's what your preview will show. But let's walk through everything you can see on this page and your other possible print options.

Print

Right at the top of the page under the Print header is the printer icon. It shows a printer and says Print under it. This is what you click when you're ready to print your document.

Copies

Next to that is where you specify the number of copies to print. By default the number to print is 1, but you can use the arrows on the right-hand side of the text box to increase that number. (Or decrease it if you've already increased it.) You can also just click into the white text box and type the number of copies you want.

Printer

Below those two options is the Printer section. This is where you specify the printer to use. It should be your default printer, but in some corporate environments you'll want to change your printer choice if, for example, you need the color printer.

To do this, click on the arrow on the right-hand side. This will bring up a dropdown menu with all of your printers listed. Click on the one you want. If the one you want isn't listed then use Add Printer to add it.

Printer Properties

You can click on the text that says Printer Properties right below that although most of the options covered there will also be covered in the Settings section on

Print Your Presentation

the main page. If you do click, the Paper/Quality tab this is where you can choose the type of paper, its source, and the quality of your print job.

Print All Slides/Print Selection/Print Current Slide/ Custom Range

Your next option is what to print. By default, you'll print all the slides in the presentation.

If you were clicked onto a specific slide in the presentation and want to just print it then you can choose Print Current Slide. (When you choose this the print preview should change to show just that one slide.)

If you had selected more than one slide in the presentation and then chose to print, you can choose Print Selection to print those slides. (You'd do that in the left-hand task pane.)

Your other option is to print a custom range. The easiest way to use this one is to type the slide numbers you want into the Slides text box directly below the dropdown. This will automatically change the dropdown selection to Custom Range. Your preview will also change to just show the slides you've listed.

You can list numbers either individually or as ranges. If you list a range you use a dash between the first and last number. So 1-10 would print slides 1 through 10. You can also use commas to separate numbers or ranges. So 1, 2, 5-12 would print slides 1, 2 and 5 through 12.

Full Page Slides/Notes Pages/Outline/Handouts

The next choice is what you want to print.

In the top section you can choose to print full page slides, notes pages, or an outline.

Full page slides will put one slide on each page you print and nothing else.

Notes pages will put one slide per page on the top half of the page and your notes on the bottom half of the page. Each page will be in portrait orientation. (Short edge on the top.)

The Outline option will take all of the text from your slides and list it out in the same way it's listed on the slides. So if there are bullet points, the outline will have them, too. If there aren't, it won't. Each printed page will contain multiple slides' worth of information. No images are included.

If you want to provide handout slides the next section gives you a number of options to choose from.

The one slide option will center each presentation slide in the middle of a page in portrait orientation. (Not recommended.) The two slide option will put two slides on each page in portrait orientation. (This is a good choice for handouts because it's still visible but doesn't waste paper the way the one-slide option does.)

You can put as many as nine slides on the page, but before you do that think about how legible that will be for the end-user. If you have a lot of slides with images it might be fine, but if they have a lot of text on them or if people will need/want to take a lot of notes, no one is going to thank you for putting nine slides on a page.

The horizontal and vertical choices determine whether the slides are ordered across and then down (horizontal) or down and then across (vertical). I think, at least in the U.S., that most people would expect horizontal.

Print One Sided/Print On Both Sides

If you want to print on both sides of the page this is where you would specify that. The default is to just print on one side of the page, but you can choose to print on both sides and either flip on the short edge or the long edge of the page.

If the paper orientation is Portrait, choose Flip on Long Edge. If the paper orientation is Landscape, choose Flip on Short Edge. For presentation slides you'll generally be working in landscape and want to flip on the short edge, but if you're printing handouts or with notes you'll generally want portrait and to flip on the long edge.

Collated/Uncollated

This only matters if you're printing more than one copy of the presentation. In that case, you need to decide if you want to print one full copy at a time x number of times (collated) or if you want to print x copies of page 1 and then x copies of page 2 and then x copies of page 3 and so on until you've printed all pages of your document (uncollated).

In general, I would recommend collated, which is also the default. In most situations I've been in the audience is given the entire presentation at the start. But if you're handing out the presentation slides one at a time then uncollated will make that easier to do.

Print Your Presentation

Portrait Orientation/Landscape Orientation

This determines whether what you've chosen to print prints with the long edge of the page at the top (landscape) or the short end of the page at the top (portrait).

In general, PowerPoint chooses this for you and does a good job of it. For example, outline should be portrait and full page slides should be landscape and PowerPoint makes that adjustment for you.

However, you might want to change this for the handout slides. For one slide, four slide, and nine slide printing, I think landscape is a better choice than portrait. You can judge for yourself by looking at the preview and seeing how large the slides are and how much white space is taken up with each orientation.

Color/Grayscale/Pure Black and White

This option lets you choose whether to print your slides in color or not. The choice you make will probably depend on your available print resources. When you change the option you'll see in the print preview what each one looks like.

The Color option will look just like your slides:

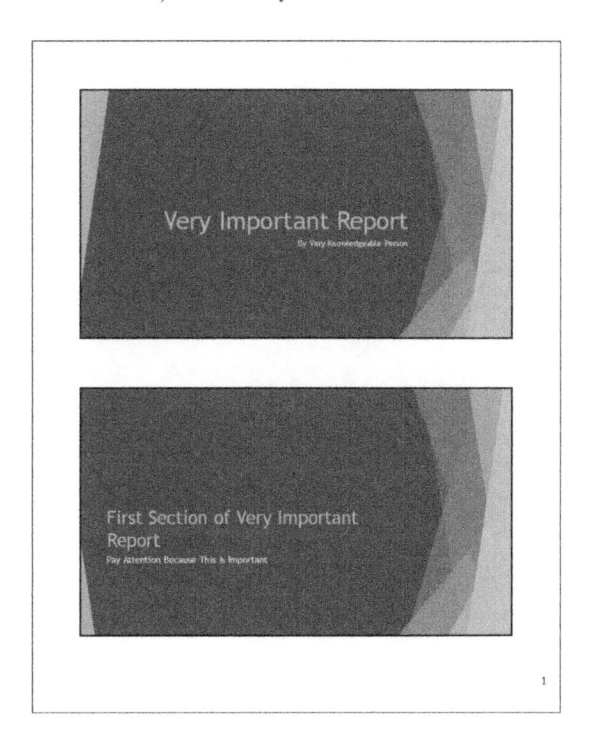

The Grayscale option will print your background elements but strips out any solid background color and converts any colors on the page and any images to grayscale.

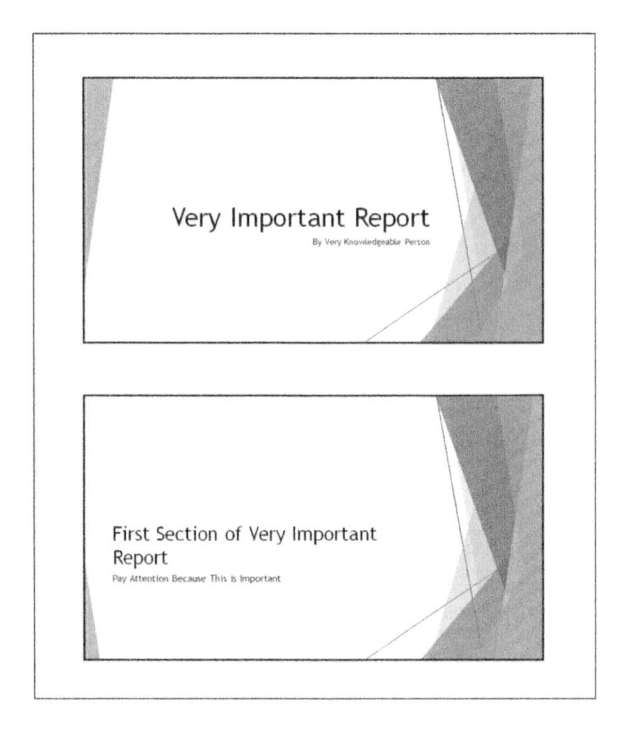

The pure black and white one looks to strip the background color as well as the color from most of the design elements. It does appear to leave images in the main body of the presentation in grayscale.

Print Your Presentation

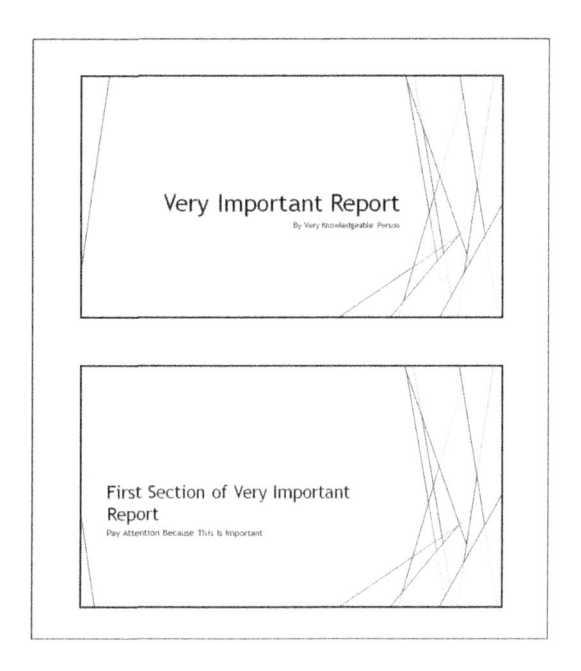

Edit Header & Footer

At the very bottom of the list you can click on the Edit Header & Footer text to bring up the Header and Footer dialogue box where you can choose to add headers or footers to your printed document. The choices available to you will depend on what you're printing.

There are separate tabs for Slides and for Notes and Handouts.

For Slides you can add the date and time, a slide number, and a footer. There is an option to not show this information for the title slide.

For Notes and Handouts you can add the date and time, page number, a header, and a footer.

Some templates will include headers and footers by default.

Once you make your choices, you can see how it will look in the print preview.

Where to Look For Other Answers

Okay, so that's what we're going to cover in this introductory guide.

My goal was to give you a solid understanding of how PowerPoint works and to lead you through the basics of creating a presentation.

There are a number of topics I didn't cover in this guide, such as how to change a presentation slide background color, creating a custom design template, adding timing to your presentation slides, adding objects or text boxes to a slide, adding charts, etc.

At some point you'll probably want to learn about one of those things.

So how do you do it? Where do you get these answers?

First, in PowerPoint itself you have a few options. You can hold your cursor over the choices in any of the tabs and you'll usually see a brief explanation of what that choice can do.

If that brief description isn't enough, a lot of the options have a Tell Me More option below that, like here for the New Slide option in the Insert tab.

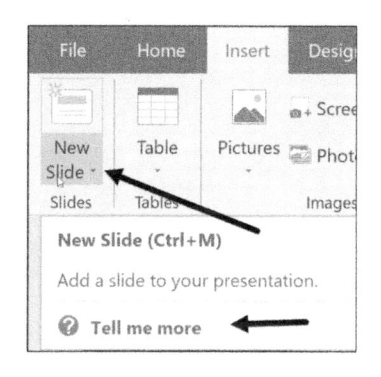

Click on Tell Me More and the built-in Help function in PowerPoint will open a task pane that provides a more detailed discussion of that option. In this example it opens a help topic titled "Add, rearrange, duplicate, and delete slides in PowerPoint" that includes a video as well as written instructions.

Another option is to go directly to the built-in Help function. You do this by clicking on the Help tab and then choosing Help again. You can also press F1.

This will open the Help task pane and you can either search for what you need or navigate through the menu options from there.

I sometimes need more information than this so turn to the internet. (More so with Word and Excel than PowerPoint, but it happens sometimes.)

If I need to know the mechanics of how something works, the Microsoft website is the best option. For example, if I wanted to understand more about the colors used in each theme in PowerPoint I might search for "colors powerpoint theme microsoft 2019".

It's key that you add the powerpoint, microsoft, and your version year in your search so that the result is relevant to your situation.

When I get my search results, I then look for a search result that goes to support.office.com. There will usually be one in the top three or four search results.

If that doesn't work or I need to know something that isn't about how things work but whether something is possible, then I will do an internet search to find a blog or user forum where someone else had the same question. Often there are good tutorials out there that you can read or watch to find your answer.

And, of course, you can also just reach out to me at mlhumphreywriter@gmail.com and I'll try to help if I can.

I'm happy to track down an answer for you or point you in the right direction. Although don't ask me to do your presentation for you. That I won't do. Or I'll do it, but I'll bill you for it.

Conclusion

So there you have it. We've covered the basics of PowerPoint and at this point in time you should be able to create your own nicely polished basic presentation.

Knowing how to create a presentation like this is a valuable skill. I've used PowerPoint presentations for small groups all the way up to rooms full of five hundred people. When you're suddenly standing in front of an audience a presentation like this can help keep you organized and focused on what you wanted to say. It also keeps you from forgetting some vital point as everyone in the room stares at you.

And having a presentation to refer to will in general make you a better presenter because you won't be staring down at a pile of notes the entire time. It also gives your audience something to look at other than you.

Just a final reminder, keep your audience in mind when creating a presentation. Most of my presentations have been given in corporate or regulatory settings, some in more creative settings. But I always live by the motto that the presentation is there to support me not distract from what I'm saying which is why I keep all the crazy shapes and garish color combinations to a minimum. (Although, even I have my weaknesses as you saw with me using the picture of my dog in this book.)

Anyway. Good luck with it. And reach out if you get stuck.

And if you want to continue to learn more about PowerPoint, check out *PowerPoint 2019 Intermediate*.

INDEX

A

Animations 89–92

    Adjust Order 90–92

    Group Text 90–92

Arrow, Definition 10

B

Bulleted Lists 69–70, 89

    Appear Separately 89

C

Click, Definition 4

Close File 19

Control Shortcut, Definition 12

Cursor, Definition 10

D

Delete File 19, 28

Design Principles 95–97, 119

Dialogue Box, Definition 7

Dropdown Menu, Definition 5

E

Expansion Arrows, Definition 6

F

Find 102

Footer 115

Format Painter 72

H

Header 115

Help 117–118

Highlight, Definition 4

L

Left-Click, Definition 4

N

New Presentation 13–14

Numbered Lists 70–72, 89

    Appear Separately 89

O

Open Presentation 15–16

P

Paragraph Formatting

    Alignment 64–66

    Columns 67

    Decrease List Level 61–62

    Hanging Indent 63

    Increase List Level 61–62

    Line Spacing 68

Pictures

    Alignment 87

    Artistic Effects 88

    Bring Forward 86

    Color 88

    Corrections 88

    Crop 85

    Insert 81–82

    Move 82

    Reset 84

    Resize 82–84

    Rotate 84

    Send Backward 86

    Styles 87

Presentation Mode 105

Presentation Size 103

Presenter View 106

Print 109–115

Q

Quick Access Toolbar, Definition 11

R

Rename File 18

Replace

    Font 103

    Text 102

Right-Click, Definition 4

S

Save Presentation 17

Scroll Bar, Definition 9–10

Select, Definition 4

Slide Show 105

Slides

    Add 25

    Copy 27

    Cut 26

    Layouts 35–43

    Move 26

    Notes 99

    Paste 27

    Reset 28

    Select 25

Spellcheck 100–101

T

Tab, Definition 3

Tables

    Add Columns 77

    Add Numbers 76

    Add Rows 77

    Add Text 76

    Align Text 77

    Banded Rows 80

    Borders 80

    Column Width 78

    Delete 78

    Delete Columns 78

    Delete Rows 78

    Design 80

    Insert 75

    Merge Cells 80

    Move 78

    Resize 79

    Row Height 79

    Split Cells 79

Task Pane, Definition 7–8

Text

    Add 45–48

    Alignment 66

    Bold 56

    Change Case 58

    Clear Formatting 59

    Copy 49

    Cut 49

    Delete 50

    Font 52–53

    Font Color 53–55

    Font Size 48, 50–52

    Indent 46–47

    Italicize 56

    Move 49

    Paste 49–50

    Underline 56–57

Themes 29–34, 40

    Colors 33

    Variants 32

U

Undo, Definition 12

W

Workspace 21–23

ABOUT THE AUTHOR

M.L. Humphrey is a former stockbroker with a degree in Economics from Stanford and an MBA from Wharton who has spent close to twenty years as a regulator and consultant in the financial services industry.

———————————

You can reach M.L. at mlhumphreywriter@gmail.com or at mlhumphrey.com.

Made in the USA
Las Vegas, NV
01 March 2025

18864950R00072